Fodor's
25 Best

PARIS

D0167874

Contents

KEY TO SYMBOLS

- ✚ Map reference to the accompanying pull-out map
- ✉ Address
- ☎ Telephone number
- ◷ Opening/closing times
- 🍴 Restaurant or café
- Ⓜ Nearest Métro (subway) station
- 🚌 Nearest bus route
- 🚆 Nearest rail station

ENTERTAINMENT 130

Whether you're after a cultural fix or just want a place to relax with a drink after a hard day's sight-seeing, we've made the best choices for you.

EAT 140

Uncover great dining experiences, from a quick bite at lunch to top-notch evening meals.

SLEEP 152

We've brought together the best hotels in the city, whatever budget you're on.

NEED TO KNOW 160

The practical information you need to make your trip run smoothly.

PULL-OUT MAP

The pull-out map with this book is a comprehensive street plan of the city. We've given grid references within the book for each sight and listing.

🚢 Nearest riverboat or ferry stop
♿ Facilities for visitors with disabilities
ℹ️ Tourist information
❓ Other practical information

💷 Admission charges:
    Expensive (over €12),
    Moderate (€6–€12) and
    Inexpensive (under €6)
▷ Further information

Introducing Paris

The City of Light needs no introduction: the Eiffel Tower, Sacré-Cœur, the Louvre. It is not a museum, however, but a vibrant urban area. The monuments won't change, but everything else will. Forget stereotypes and see the city with new eyes.

Paris has been making a concerted effort to change its image as a cold city full of rude, arrogant people. That reputation was never entirely deserved, but the good news for both visitors and residents is that Paris has undergone many changes for the better. The mayor's office and the national government sponsor a number of popular (and free) annual events along the lines of the *Fête de la Musique* (21 June), which bring the normally reserved Parisians out to have fun.

In addition to *Paris Plages*, when the Right Bank of the Seine becomes a sandy beach for one month in the summer, the city is the site of *La Nuit des Musées* (May), when several museums stay open all night; *Les Journées du Patrimoine* (September), when normally off-limits monuments are open; *La Nuit Blanche* (October), with all-night art and cultural events; and outdoor music concerts in the summer.

And Paris is no longer deserted in August. Once transformed into a quiet village while the entire working population holidayed elsewhere, the city has come back to life as the French learn to stagger their holidays. It's still quiet, but more and more restaurants and shops are open. Picnicking in the city is now popular and the banks of the Seine and parks are full of outdoor diners. The once-forbidden lawns in its parks and squares are packed with children and sunbathers.

Most visitors come to see the great monuments, however. Having miraculously survived wars and revolution—some of them for a thousand years—they now seem to be eternal.

In recent years, much effort has gone into improving the quality of life in Paris, with projects like the Vélib' bicycle hire scheme (▷ 167) and *Paris Plages* enjoyed by Parisians and visitors alike.

FACTS AND FIGURES

- Population: 2.2 million
- Area: 105 sq km (40.5 sq miles)
- GDP (Île de France): €631 billion
- Highest elevation: Montmartre at 128m (420ft)
- Mayor: Anne Hildago (Socialist)
- Divided into 20 *arrondissements*
- Eiffel Tower: The tower has 2.5 million rivets and is lit by 20,000 light bulbs

FLIGHT OF FANCY

The first manned flight took place in Paris when Pilatre de Rozier and the Marquis d'Arlandes made a 25-minute trip in a hot-air balloon from the Bois de Boulogne to what is now the 13th *arrondissement* on 21 November 1783. Among the crowd observing their feat was none other than Benjamin Franklin, one of the founding fathers of the USA.

CLOSED

Every Tuesday a crowd of disappointed tourists gathers outside the closed entrance to the Louvre pyramid. Remember that most major museums are closed one day a week: Monday for the city-run museums (such as the Musée Carnavalet and Musée d'Art Moderne de la Ville de Paris) and Tuesday for national museums (including the Louvre, Centre Pompidou and Grand Palais).

DID YOU KNOW?

● Every evening, nearly 300 Parisian monuments, hotels, churches, fountains, bridges and canals are illuminated against the night sky.
● France has banned smoking inside restaurants, bars and cafés, for the dining pleasure of all.
● Watch your step! In spite of the city's best efforts to alleviate the problem, dog droppings are still a hazard.

Focus On Paris On Screen

Few places are as closely associated with the film industry as Paris, the birthplace of cinema and a city whose many charms have been embedded in the world's imagination through the movies.

Birth of a New Medium

The history of modern cinema began properly in Paris on 28 December 1895, in the Salon Indien of the Grand Café on the boulevard des Capucines. At this venue, the Lumière brothers, Louis and Auguste, first demonstrated the potential of their invention, the *cinématographe*—a portable camera, film processing unit and projector combined—by screening 10 of their short films to a paying audience. The first film they showed was *La Sortie des Usines Lumière*, a simple shot of workers leaving the family's factory in Lyon. It lasted less than a minute, yet the public response was immediate and enthusiastic. A new entertainment medium had hit the scene, paving the way for one of the most influential and commercial entertainment genres for future generations.

The Parisian Scene

Throughout cinema history, Paris itself has been one of the great stars of the silver screen. In the 1926 silent film *Paris*, Charles Ray fell for Joan Crawford in the louche setting of the Paris Apache (pronounced Ah-Pahsh) or demi-monde, the era of hedonistic lifestyles and decadent jazz clubs. The Apaches were originally Paris members of street gangs, and later the name was used for a new dance. In the 1950s, a string of big-budget Hollywood movies, from *An American in Paris* (1951) to *Funny Face* (1957), peddled the image of Paris as the capital of love and romance to a receptive international audience, with gamine European actresses like Leslie Caron and Audrey

Clockwise from top: La Pagode cinema in rue de Babylone; Le Champo cinema in rue des Écoles; a scene from An American in Paris, *1951; Les Deux*

Hepburn personifying its elegance and fashion sense. In *Sabrina* (1954), Hepburn can be seen composing a letter to the wistful tune of "La Vie en Rose" as the Sacré-Cœur is seen through an open window. The film and its content may only ever have been an outsider's ideal of the City of Light, but as myths go it was a potent one. Hepburn was a Parisian *ingénue* in *Love in the Afternoon* (1957) and returned for *Paris When It Sizzles* (1964), though by then, perhaps, the formula had become a little stale.

Beyond the Romance

Inevitably, the depiction of Paris in French cinema has been somewhat less starry-eyed. Jean-Luc Godard's *Breathless* (*À bout de souffle*; 1960) may have had the relationship between Jean-Paul Belmondo and Jean Seberg at its core, but this *nouvelle vague* masterpiece is no sugar-coated romance. François Truffaut's *The Last Metro* (1980) dealt with the perils of the German occupation, Cyril Collard's *Savage Nights* (1992) with the complications of love in a time of AIDS. But French cinema is not immune to the capital's charms either, as Jean-Pierre Jeunet's magical, color-saturated *Amélie* (2001) proved to huge international success. The film featured Audrey Tautou as a shy waitress in a Montmartre café and Paris itself— as enchanting as in any 1950s musical—was her co-star.

The Tradition Maintained

Paris has remained true to its early passion for film. Director Luc Besson's project for La Cité du Cinéma (City of Cinema), which opened in 2012, has brought 45,000 sq m (484,400 sq ft) of film production space to a former power station in the northern suburb of Saint-Denis. The impact of film on the city comes full circle.

Moulins café, setting for the film Amélie, *2001; a poster for the Lumière brothers' new world of cinema; at work on* Paris When it Sizzles, *1964*

Top Tips For...

These great suggestions will help you tailor your ideal visit to Paris, no matter how you choose to spend your time. Each sight or listing has a fuller write-up elsewhere in the book.

Antiquing
Hunt for a bargain at the **Marché aux Puces de Saint-Ouen** (▷ 26–27), an immense weekend flea market.
Put in a bid for the unique items at **Drouot Richelieu auction house** (▷ 67).
Visit the warren of antiques shops at the **Louvre des Antiquaires** (▷ 127).

Haute Couture
Find a wide selection of designer clothing at the department stores **Le Bon Marché Rive Gauche** (▷ 123), **Galeries Lafayette** or **Printemps** (▷ 126, panel).
Try on original yet timeless styles at **Colette** (▷ 124): it's cutting-edge and very exclusive.
Top off your look with one of **Marie Mercié's** fabulous hats (▷ 128).

Fine Dining
Check out the Michelin-starred **Gordon Ramsay au Trianon** (▷ 148), a luxurious dining experience on a trip to Versailles.
Find out how **Guy Savoy** turns cooking into an art form at his eponymous restaurant (▷ 149).
Put yourself in the hands of chef Eric Frechon and try his tasting menu at **Epicure** (▷ 148).

All-Night Antics
Spot the celebs at trendy club **Le Baron** (▷ 135).
Drink martinis into the wee hours in the old-fashioned New World ambience of **Harry's New York Bar** (▷ 137).
Gasp at the high-kicking routines at **Le Crazy Horse** cabaret show (▷ 136–137).

Clockwise from top: A market stall at the Marché aux Puces de Saint-Ouen; relaxing in the Jardin du Luxembourg; admiring art in the Musée Carnavalet;

Descend into the medieval basement at **Caveau de la Huchette** for jazz (▷ 136). Take in a concert at the **Divan du Monde** (▷ 137) and stay on afterwards to hear some great guest DJs.

Catering to the Kids
Ride the glass elevator to the top of the **Eiffel Tower** (▷ 60–61).
Explore interactive exhibitions at the **Cité des Sciences et de l'Industrie** in the Parc de la Villette (▷ 76).
Set the little darlings loose in the **Si Tu Veux** toy shop (▷ 129).

Shoestring Pleasures
Take advantage of free admission to the permanent collections of all city-run museums: the **Musée Carnavalet** (▷ 28–29), **Musée d'Art Moderne de la Ville de Paris** (▷ 70) and many more.
Visit the **Atelier Brancusi**, a reconstruction of sculptor Constantin Brancusi's workshop, in front of the **Centre Georges Pompidou** (▷ 16–17), for free.

Bird's-Eye Views
Stop shopping long enough to check out the view from **Printemps de la Maison's** ninth floor (▷ 126, panel).
Take in the view from central Paris's only sky-scraper, the **Tour Montparnasse** (▷ 75).
Eat in the Eiffel Tower's **Le Jules Verne** restaurant (▷ 149) for fine food with views.

Lazy Mornings
Cruise leisurely down the Seine in a *bateau mouche* (▷ 58–59).
Commune with the ghosts of Sartre and Hemingway at the **Café de Flore** (▷ 66).
Sit by the fountain in the **Domaine Nationale du Palais Royal** (▷ 66–67) with a book by Colette, who once lived there.

Harry's New York Bar in rue Daunou; the impressive glass dome of the prestigious Galeries Lafayette department store

Timeline

BEFORE 1000

● The Celtic tribe of Parisii settles on Île de la Cité around 200BC.
● By AD100 the Roman city of Lutetia, later Paris, is growing fast.
● In 451 Sainte Geneviève saves Paris from the threat of Attila the Hun.

1163 The building of Notre-Dame starts.

1337–1453 Hundred Years' War between France and England.

1431 Henry VI of England is crowned king of France in Notre-Dame.

1437 Charles VII regains control of Paris.

1572 St. Bartholomew Massacre occurs during the Wars of Religion.

1682 Louis XIV and the court move to Versailles.

1700s Intellectuals, including Rousseau and Diderot, introduce radical new ideas during the Age of Enlightenment.

1789 Storming of the Bastille.

1792 Monarchy abolished; proclamation of the Republic.

1804 Napoleon crowned emperor.

1830 Bourbons overthrown; Louis-Philippe crowned.

1848 Revolution topples Louis-Philippe; Second Republic headed by Napoleon III, who is later crowned emperor.

REIGN OF TERROR

From 1793 to 1794 the Reign of Terror seized France, masterminded by the ruthless, power-crazed Jacobin leaders Robespierre and Danton. The king, Louis XVI, was convicted of treason and guillotined in January 1793, followed in October by his queen, Marie-Antoinette. By mid-1794 more than 18,000 people are estimated to have been beheaded in France.

The gardens at the Château de Versailles

The Consecration of the Emperor Napoleon, *by Jacques-Louis David*

1852–70 Baron Haussmann oversees the transformation of Paris.

1870–71 Paris besieged by Prussians, civil uprising of the Commune, Republic restored.

1889 Eiffel Tower is completed.

1900 First Métro line opens.

1914–18 Paris bombarded by German cannon.

1940 Nazis occupy Paris, followed by Liberation in 1944.

1958 De Gaulle heads Fifth Republic.

1977 Jacques Chirac is elected mayor (then president in 1995). Centre Georges Pompidou opens.

1981 Election of President Mitterrand. He initiates his *Grands Projets*—a new building scheme.

2002 First *Paris Plage*, in which riverside roads are closed in summer to create an urban beach on the banks of the Seine.

2014 Anne Hidalgo is elected the first female mayor of the city.

2015 Terrorist attacks in January at the Charlie Hebdo offices and then across the city in November shock the city, but around 1.6 million people march through the streets of Paris in defense of liberty.

2016 France hosts Euro 2016 football tournament with the final in Paris.

The Liberation of Paris, 1944

THE SEINE

The city's history has been inextricably linked with the River Seine, which snakes its way through the city, since its earliest origins as a Gaulish village on the Île de la Cité, an islet in the river. The Seine represents the very lifeblood of Paris, flowing through its heart, animating the city, defining the capital geographically and reflecting its history in its many fine buildings. After centuries of pollution—when the river was used as a sewer—the Seine has been cleaned and its water is less polluted than it has been for years, although it's probably not a good idea to jump in for a swim.

TOP 25 Top 25

This section contains the must-see Top 25 sights and experiences in Paris. They are listed alphabetically, and numbered so you can locate them on the inside front cover.

● Views from the terrace
● *La Marseillaise*, François Rude
● Tomb of the Unknown Soldier

TIP

● The museum has audio-visual displays illustrating major historical events and the construction of the Arc.

At the hub of Haussmann's web of 12 avenues, which reach out like tentacles towards the city beyond, this is the ultimate symbol of Napoleon's military pretensions and might. Climb the 284 steps to the terrace for superb views.

National symbol Napoleon conceived the Arc de Triomphe as a symbol of his military might in 1806 but it was finished only in 1836 by Louis-Philippe. Two centuries on and the colossal monument is still an iconic image of national pride. It plays a central role in many of France's key commemorations, including VE Day (8 May), Bastille Day (14 July) and Remembrance Day (11 November). Within its grounds are the Tomb of the Unknown Soldier, installed in 1921 after World War I, and a

Clockwise from far left: The Arc de Triomphe at dusk; the Tomb of the Unknown Soldier beneath the monument; view of the Arc from the esplanade de la Défense; looking towards the Eiffel Tower; roll call of French generals, etched into the inside walls

poignant Memorial Flame, added two years later. This flame is rekindled every evening.

Special interest There are wonderful views from the rooftop, 50m (164ft) high. From here you can admire Haussmann's weblike street design and look along the Grand Axis toward place de la Concorde in one direction and the Grande Arche in the other. There is a small shop and museum on the way up. At ground level, save time to admire the magnificent sculpted facade, the work of three artists. Don't miss the winged figure of Liberty on François Rude's sculpture *La Marseillaise*, calling the French to defend their nation (northeastern pillar, facing the Champs-Élysées). The 30 shields studding the crown of the arch each bear the name of a Revolutionary or Imperial victory.

THE BASICS

arc-de-triomphe.
monuments-nationaux.fr

➕ B2

✉ Place Charles-de-Gaulle, 75008

☎ 01 55 37 73 77

🕐 Apr–Sep daily 10am–11pm; Oct–Mar 10am–10.30pm. Times may vary. Last admission 45 mins before closing

Ⓜ Charles de Gaulle–Étoile

🚌 22, 30, 31, 52, 73, 92, Balabus

♿ Moderate

HIGHLIGHTS

● Design by Sir Richard Rogers, Renzo Piano and Jean-François Bodin
● View from the escalator
● Stravinsky fountain
● Trendy and cool design in Georges restaurant
● Avant-premières of new films and retrospectives of the work of top cinema directors
● Design shop on level 1

TIP

● Lines for tickets can be long; cut waiting times by booking in advance online.

Late opening hours make an exhibition visit possible between an *apéritif* and dinner in this still-controversial cultural area. You can take your pick between the genesis of modernism, an art film or a drama performance.

High-tech culture More than a mere landmark in the extensive face-lift that Paris has undergone since the 1970s, the high-tech Centre Pompidou (known to Parisians as Beaubourg) is a hive of changing cultural activity. Contemporary art, architecture, design, photography, theater, cinema and dance are all represented, while the lofty structure offers exceptional views over central Paris. Take the transparent escalator tubes for a bird's-eye view of the piazza, where jugglers, artists, musicians and portrait artists perform for the crowds.

Clockwise from far left: The inside-out exterior of the building; detail of the Stravinsky fountain outside the Centre; futuristic features on the exterior; glass corridor with fine views over the city; the Centre viewed above the rooftops of the city; more pipes and structures on the facade

TOP 25

Classic modernism The Musée National d'Art Moderne's permanent collections feature work from 1905 to the 1960s on the fifth floor, with works from the contemporary collection on level four. Items displayed from the 59,000-strong collection change regularly and range from cubism by Georges Braque to Pop Art by Andy Warhol and video art by Korean artist Nam June Paik. For a chronological overview start on the fifth floor. Levels 1, 4 and 6 are for temporary exhibitions, while a public information library is on levels 1, 2 and 3. The ground level includes a bookshop and museum boutique (there are other bookstands on levels 4 and 6), a post office and a children's workshop. There are cinemas on the first and lower floors and the restaurant Georges, with its wonderful views over the city, is on the top floor.

THE BASICS

centrepompidou.fr

➕ K5

✉ Place Georges-Pompidou, 75004

☎ 01 44 78 12 33

🕐 Museum and exhibits Wed–Mon 11–10. Last tickets 8. Atelier Brancusi (▷ 9) Wed–Mon 2–6. Library Mon, Wed–Fri 12–10, Sat–Sun 11–10

🍴 Georges restaurant on 6th floor; café

🚇 Rambuteau, Hôtel de Ville

🚌 29, 38, 39, 47, 58, 67, 75, 76, 81

🚆 RER Line A, B, Châtelet–Les Halles

♿ Excellent

💲 Expensive

HIGHLIGHTS

- Marie-Antoinette's cell
- Tour Bonbec
- Prisoners' cells upstairs

TIP

● If you also plan to visit Sainte-Chapelle (▷ 56–57), go to the Conciergerie first and buy a joint ticket, to avoid the lines at Sainte-Chapelle. But do try to get to Sainte-Chapelle in the morning, before it gets very busy.

The ghosts of the victims of the guillotine must surely haunt this stark and gloomy place that served as a prison and torture chamber for more than five centuries and remains full of macabre mementoes of its grisly past.

From palace to prison Rising over the Seine in menacing grandeur, the Conciergerie was built from 1299 to 1313 as part of a royal complex that also included Sainte-Chapelle. From 1391 until 1914 the building functioned as a prison and torture chamber, its reputation striking fear in the population. During the Revolution more than 2,700 people appeared before the Revolutionary Tribunal at the Conciergerie, including Marie-Antoinette and Maximilien Robespierre.

Clockwise from top left: The beautiful Conciergerie graces the banks of the Seine; detail of the building flanked by trees; the impressive clock on the Tour de l'Horloge; representation of the clerk's room; the moody lighting enhances the Salle des Gens d'Armes

Relive history The boulevard du Palais entrance takes you into the hauntingly lit Salle des Gens d'Armes. This rib-vaulted hall is considered one of the finest examples of secular Gothic architecture in Europe. The curious spiral staircase on the right of the hall once led to the Great Ceremonial Hall on the upper floor of the palace. Off the Salle des Gens d'Armes is the gloomy Salle des Gardes; this acted as an antechamber to the now-vanished Grand'Chambre on the upper floor, where the Revolutionary Tribunal sat in 1793. Across the corridor known as the rue de Paris is the Galerie des Prisonniers, where lawyers, prisoners and visitors mingled. Here is a re-creation of the concierge's and clerk's offices, as well as the Salle de Toilette, where prisoners were prepared for execution. At the far end is a poignant re-creation of Marie-Antoinette's cell.

THE BASICS

conciergerie.monuments-nationaux.fr

✚ J6

✉ 2 boulevard du Palais, Île de la Cité, 75001

☎ 01 53 40 60 80

🕑 Daily 9.30–6 (ticket office 5.30); times may vary

Ⓜ Cité, Châtelet

🚌 21, 24, 27, 38, 58, 70, 81, 85, 96

♿ Moderate (joint ticket with Sainte-Chapelle expensive)

❓ Guided tours Wed 2.30 and Sat 10.30

Galerie Vivienne and the Passages Couverts

HIGHLIGHTS

● Mosaic floor, Galerie Vivienne
● Stamp dealers
● La Galerie Fayet
● Vintage children's books
● Decor, Le Grand Colbert

Centered on the 2nd *arrondissement* is a hidden network of interconnecting 19th-century shopping arcades or *passages couverts* that enable you to stroll under cover most of the way from the Palais Royal to the Grands Boulevards and beyond.

Galerie Vivienne Between the late 18th and early 19th centuries the Right Bank included a network of 140 covered passageways—the fashionable shopping malls of the time. Of those that survive, the Galerie Vivienne (1823) is perhaps the most glamorous, squeezed in between the Bibliothèque Nationale and the place des Victoires. You can track down designer clothes—Jean-Paul Gaultier was one of the first to open a shop here—or shop for unusual toys. It's perfect for a rainy day.

Clockwise from far left: Style and elegance feature in the Galerie Vivienne; taking a break in the café; the elaborate entrance; a superb ornate clock embellishes the wall; a nod to the present with this modern sign at the Galerie

Galerie Colbert Galerie Vivienne's nearby neighbor Galerie Colbert (1826) is as elegant, but lacks shops as it is part of the Institut National de l'Histoire de l'Art. Don't miss the 19th-century brasserie, Le Grand Colbert.

More offbeat browsing These interlinked arcades thread their way north from rue Saint-Marc across the boulevard de Montmartre and into the 9th *arrondissement*. The labyrinthine Passage des Panoramas (1800) is a little down-at-heel in places but full of inexpensive restaurants and stamp dealers. Facing it across boulevard de Montmartre is the Passage Jouffroy (1845), where the quirkiest of the boutiques, La Galerie Fayet, sells antique walking canes. Farther north still, the quieter Passage Verdeau (1847) has vintage book dealers.

THE BASICS

galerie-vivienne.com
passagedespanoramas.fr
passagejouffroy.com
➕ H4–H3
✉ Galerie Vivienne: 4 rue des Petits-Champs/6 rue Vivienne, 75002.
Passage des Panoramas: 10 rue Saint-Marc, 75002
🚇 Bourse, Palais-Royal, Grands Boulevards
🚌 20, 29, 39, 48, 67, 74, 85
♿ Good
🎫 Free

HIGHLIGHTS

- Médicis fountain
- Musée du Luxembourg
- Bandstand
- Statue of Delacroix
- Orangerie
- Experimental orchard
- Beekeeping school
- Statues of queens of France

Despite the crowds, these gardens are serene in all weathers and are the epitome of French landscaping. This idealized image of an unhurried Parisian existence is a world away from the big-city bustle nearby.

Layout Radiating from the large octagonal pond in front of the Palais du Luxembourg (now the Senate) are terraces, paths and a wide tree-lined alley that leads down to the Observatory crossroads. Natural attractions include shady chestnuts, potted orange and palm trees, an orchard and tropical hothouses. Statues of the queens of France and artists and writers are dotted about.

Park activities All year round joggers pound the circumference and in summer sunbathers

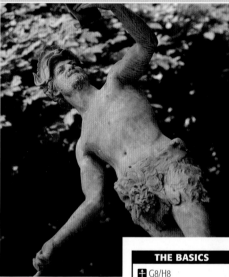

Clockwise from far left: Strolling in front of the Palais du Luxembourg; detail of the Médicis fountain; relaxing in the gardens; bronze statue, l'Acteur Grec, by Charles-Arthur Bourgeois; the gardens provide the perfect setting for a game of chess

and bookworms settle into park chairs, card- and chess-players claim the shade in front of the Orangerie, bands tune up at the bandstand near the boulevard Saint-Michel entrance and children burn off energy on swings and donkey rides. Fountains, tennis courts, beehives, a puppet theater and children's playgrounds offer other distractions. In the northwest corner of the park is Paris's oldest public museum, the Musée du Luxembourg. Opened in 1750, it became the first contemporary art museum in 1818 and today stages major temporary exhibitions of art.

Inspiration The Palais du Luxembourg and gardens were commissioned by Marie de Médicis, wife of Henri IV, in 1615, and designed to resemble her childhood Florentine home.

THE BASICS

➕ G8/H8
✉ Main entrance place Edmond Rostand, 75006
☎ Park 01 42 34 20 00. Musée du Luxembourg 01 40 13 62 00, museedu-luxembourg.fr
🕐 Park daylight hours. Museum daily 10–7.30 (10pm Mon and Fri)
🍴 Open-air café, kiosk
Ⓜ Odéon
🚌 58, 82, 84, 85, 87, 89, 93 (to museum)
🚆 RER Line B, Luxembourg
♿ Very good
💵 Park free; museum expensive

HIGHLIGHTS

- Jeu de Paume
- Orangerie
- Outdoor sculptures
- Views

Forming a verdant link between the Louvre and the Champs Elysées, the Jardin des Tuileries is perhaps Paris's most visited green space. Here history meets contemporary life as office workers eat lunch and families relax amongst the fine formal gardens that started life as a private park for the French royal family.

Good views It's also a place from where the city's visitors can see several of the city's main attractions. There are good views of the Louvre, the Eiffel Tower, the Musée d'Orsay across the river and up to the Arc de Triomphe at the top of the Champs-Élysées.

Design notes The formal design of the gardens can be credited to the landscape

Clockwise from left: The huge Ferris wheel offers wonderful views of Paris; the boating lake is popular with children; a stroll in the gardens is a great way to spend a few hours and see the outdoor art

architect André le Nôtre, who was gardener to King Louis XIV and the man responsible for the spectacular gardens at Versailles. Le Nôtre laid out the Tuileries in 1664, and over 300 years later they are still being enjoyed.

Activities In one corner is a boating pond, and at the opposite end, overlooking the place de la Concorde, are two of the city's finest small galleries, the Orangerie (▷ 51) and the Jeu de Paume (▷ 51). The latter gets its name from the fact that it was once a real tennis court *(jeu de paume)* and the former a warm winter home for the orange trees from the Jardin. There is plenty of outdoor art in the gardens, too. Works by Giacometti, Rodin and Henry Moore are on display, along with several bronzes by Aristide Maillol.

THE BASICS

- F4–5/G4–5
- ✉ 113 rue de Rivoli, 75001
- 🕐 Jun–Aug daily 7am–11pm; Apr–May, Sep 7am–9pm; Oct–Mar 7.30–7.30
- 🍴 Cafés
- Ⓜ Tuileries
- 🚌 24, 42, 68, 72, 73, 84
- ♿ Good
- 🎫 Free

HIGHLIGHTS

● Marché Serpette: art, high-quality furniture
● Marché Paul Bert: trendy items, including classic modern furniture
● Marché Jules Vallès: bric-a-brac
● Marché Biron: antiques, glass, art deco

TIP

● The market area is very extensive, so pick up a free map from the tourist office at 7 impasse Simon by the Marché Paul Bert.

A Sunday pastime popular with many locals is to look for bargains at the city's flea markets, of which the *crème de la crème* is still this one. Nowhere else will you find such a fascinating cross section of Parisian society.

Duck and banter The approach from the Métro station to this sprawling 7ha (17-acre) market is uninspiring as it entails bypassing jeans and sportswear stalls before ducking under the Périphérique overpass and finally entering the fray. Persevere and you may discover an antique gem, a fake or a secondhand item. If your budget won't stretch to that, you can choose an old postcard of Paris from the thousands on show. Everything and anything is displayed here and all commerce is carried on in the true bantering style of the *faubourgs*.

Clockwise from far left: Antiques and curiosities at the market; browse the books at Zoppa & Zoppa; pretty antique basin for sale; collector's items include an array of soda siphons; intricate carving is a feature of French furniture

It pays to get "creatively lost," since the most intriguing vendors are not necessarily the ones with the most prominent sites. In particular, don't miss the upper level if you're visiting the Marché Dauphine.

Bargain hard Registered dealers are divided into more than a dozen official markets, which interconnect through busy passageways. Along the fringes are countless hopefuls who set up temporary stands to sell goods ranging from obsolete kitchenware to old jukeboxes and junk. Although unashamedly a tourist trap, there is something for everyone here, but do go early. Bargaining is obligatory. Stop for lunch in one of the bistros along the rue des Rosiers or try the terrace of the café-theater A Picolo at 58 rue Jules-Vallès, which has occasional jazz concerts.

THE BASICS

marcheauxpuces-saintouen.com

➕ See map ▷ 115

✉ Porte de Clignancourt, 75018

☎ 01 40 11 77 36

🕐 Sat 9–6, Sun 10–6, Mon 10–5 (reduced hours in Aug)

🍽 Cafés and restaurants on rue des Rosiers

🚇 Porte de Clignancourt

🚌 56, 60, 85, 95, 137, 166, 255

♿ Good

❓ Beware of pickpockets

HIGHLIGHTS

- Statue of Louis XV
- Le Brun's ceiling painting
- *Destruction of the Bastille*, Hubert Robert
- Bastille prison keys
- Proust's bedroom
- Ballroom from the Hôtel de Wendel
- Napoleon's traveling case
- Archaeological collection in the Orangerie
- Formal garden in La Cour de la Victoire
- Robespierre's last letter

There is no better museum than this to plunge you into the history of Paris, and the renovated mansion in which it is set is hard to beat. Period rooms, objects, documents and paintings combine to illustrate the city's long and turbulent past.

Ornamental excess This captivating collection is displayed within adjoining 16th- and 17th-century town houses. The main entrance is through the superb courtyard of the Hôtel Carnavalet (1548), once the home of the celebrated writer Madame de Sévigné. Here attention focuses on the Middle Ages, the Renaissance and the decorative excess reached under Louis XIV, Louis XV and Louis XVI. Some of the richly painted and sculpted interiors are original to the building; others, such as the

Clockwise from far left: The magnificent entrance to the Hôtel Carnavalet, now home to the museum; art and architecture inside the museum; George Fouquet's jewelry boutique, designed by Alphonse Mucha; splendid topiary in the museum gardens

wood panels from the Hôtel Colbert de Villacerf and Brunetti's trompe-l'œil staircase paintings, have been brought in.

Revolution to the present Next door, the renovated Hôtel Le Peletier de Saint-Fargeau (1688) exhibits remarkable objects from the Revolution—a period when anything and everything was emblazoned with slogans—and continues with Napoleon I's dictatorship, the Restoration, the Second Empire, the Commune and finally the Belle Époque. Figures such as Robespierre and Madame de Récamier come to life within their chronological context. The collection ends in the early 20th century with fine reconstructions of interiors, including the bedroom of Marcel Proust, who, owing to severe asthma, was often confined to bed.

THE BASICS

carnavalet.paris.fr

➕ L6

✉ 23 rue de Sévigné, 75003 (entrance at 16 rue des Francs-Bourgeois)

☎ 01 44 59 58 58

🕐 Tue–Sat 10–6

Ⓢ Saint-Paul

🚌 29, 69, 76, 96

♿ Carnavalet: few; Le Peletier: good

🎫 Free; temporary exhibitions moderate

HIGHLIGHTS

- Palace of Khorsabad
- Glass pyramid entrance, designed by I.M. Pei
- *Bataille de San Romano*, Uccello
- *Mona Lisa*, da Vinci
- Napoleon III apartments
- Vénus de Milo
- Cour Carrée at night
- The Marly Horses

TIP

- To avoid the crowds, visit early morning or Wednesday or Friday evening.

Nocturnal lighting transforms the Louvre's glass pyramid entrance into a gigantic cut diamond—just a foretaste of the treasures contained within.

The world's largest museum Originally a medieval fortress, the Louvre first took shape as a private art gallery under François I, eager to display his Italian loot. Henri IV added several galleries, completed in 1610. After escaping the excesses of the Revolutionary mob, it became a people's museum in 1793 and was later enlarged by Napoleon I, who also enriched its collection. Today the Louvre remains a vibrant and exciting art gallery, while its star attraction, the iconic *Mona Lisa,* hangs in its own room which has been specially refurbished to make viewing the painting easier.

Clockwise from far left: All glass and light, the interior of the Louvre; a view across the fountains to the famous glass pyramid; The Raft of the Medusa by Théodore Géricault; detail of the glass pyramid; sculptures in the Richelieu Wing

Art fortress The vast collection of some 35,000 exhibits is arranged on four floors of three wings: Sully (east), Richelieu (north) and Denon (south), while beneath the elegant Cour Carrée lies the keep of the original medieval fortress. Almost 5,000 years of art are covered at the museum, starting with Egyptian antiquities and culminating with European painting up to 1848. Islamic art from three continents is showcased in a contemporary space within the Cour Visconti.

Making the most of your visit There is no way that you'll be able to see everything in one visit, so you'll need to be selective. The free museum map, available from the information desk, highlights the key works and is useful when planning your visit.

THE BASICS

louvre.fr

➕ H5

✉ 99 rue de Rivoli, 75058. Enter via Pyramid or Carrousel

☎ 01 40 20 50 50; Auditorium 01 40 20 55 55

🕐 Wed–Mon 9–6 (until 9.45pm Wed, Fri)

🍴 Restaurants and cafés

Ⓜ Palais-Royal–Musée du Louvre

🚍 21, 24, 27, 39, 48, 68, 69, 72, 81, 95

♿ Excellent

💷 Expensive; temporary exhibitions expensive; free first Sun of month Oct–Mar

❓ Tours, audio guides, lectures, films, workshops, concerts. Buy your ticket online to save a long wait

The Marmottan Monet Museum, in the residential 16th *arrondissement*, houses a mesmerizing collection of Monet paintings, including many colorful canvases of the artist's home in Giverny.

Rich donations This often overlooked treasure of Parisian culture offers an eclectic collection built up over the years from the original donation of Renaissance and First Empire paintings and furniture bequeathed by the art historian Paul Marmottan in 1932. His elegant 19th-century mansion, furnished with Renaissance tapestries and sculptures and Napoleonic furniture, was later given an extra boost by the stunning Wildenstein collection of 313 pages from illustrated manuscripts from the 13th to the 16th centuries, as well as an exceptional

Clockwise from far left: An elegant room used to display Impressionist paintings; visitors admiring the works of Claude Monet and his contemporaries

donation from Michel Monet of works by his father Claude, the Impressionist painter. Other generous donations include works by Monet's contemporaries Gauguin, Renoir, Boudin, Pissarro, Sisley, Berthe Morisot and Gustave Caillebotte, but it is Monet's canvases of dappled irises, wisteria and water lilies, from his last years at Giverny, that are among the most sought out and memorable.

Visiting the museum The museum shop and Salons Impressionnistes are on the ground floor. You will find more Impressionists and the Salle Monet in the basement, while the Wildenstein collection of illuminated manuscripts is housed in a specially designed room. The museum also stages regular temporary exhibitions on themes related to its collections.

THE BASICS

marmottan.fr
➕ See map ▷ 114
✉ 2 rue Louis-Boilly, 75016
☎ 01 44 96 50 33
🕐 Tue–Sun 10–6 (Thu until 9). Last admission 30 mins before closing.
🚇 La Muette
🚌 22, 32, 52, 63
🚆 RER Line C, Boulainvilliers
♿ Moderate

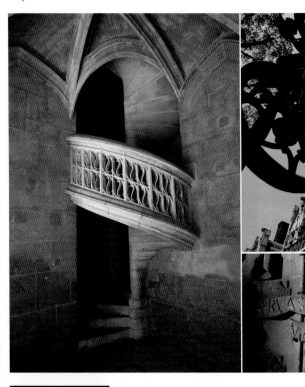

HIGHLIGHTS

- *La Dame à la Licorne*
  (The Lady and the Unicorn)
  tapestries
- Gold altar frontal
- *Pilier des Nautes*
- Stone heads from
  Notre-Dame
- Medieval gardens
- Seventh-century votive
  crown
- Stained glass
- Abbot's Chapel

Take a deep breath outside this museum, surrounded by re-created medieval gardens, and prepare to enter a time warp that conjures up the days of troubadours and courtly love.

Treasures The Gothic turreted Hôtel de Cluny was built at the end of the 15th century by Abbot Jacques d'Amboise and is one of France's finest examples of domestic architecture of this period. The museum it houses, also known as the Musée de Cluny, has 23,000 objects in its collection, most amassed by Alexandre du Sommerard, a 19th-century medievalist. The most famous exhibits are the beautiful *La Dame à la Licorne* tapestries (late 15th century). Costumes, accessories, textiles and tapestries are of Byzantine, Coptic or European

Clockwise from far left: Stone staircase, bathed in lights, in the Gothic Hôtel de Cluny; exterior of the building, now housing the museum; detail of a religious painting displayed in the museum; exterior courtyard, once the site of ancient Roman baths; detail of shells on the exterior

origin, while the gold and metalwork room has outstanding pieces of Gallic, Barbarian, Merovingian and Visigothic artistry. Room VIII houses 21 stone heads knocked from statues on the west front of Notre-Dame. Stained glass, table games, ceramics, wood carvings, illuminated manuscripts and Books of Hours, altarpieces and religious statuary complete this exceptional display.

Baths The late-Roman baths of Lutetia, which comprise cold (frigidarium), tepid (tepidarium) and hot (caldarium) rooms, form part of the museum complex. The most substantial surviving element is the frigidarium, whose 14.7m (48ft) vaulted ceiling, restored in 2009, makes it one of the most important structures from antiquity to survive north of the Loire.

THE BASICS

musee-moyenage.fr

✚ J7

✉ 6 place Paul-Painlevé, 75005

☎ 01 53 73 78 00

🕔 Wed–Mon 9.15–5.45. Last admission 30 mins before closing.

🚇 Cluny–La Sorbonne

🚍 21, 27, 38, 63, 85, 86, 87

🚉 RER Line B, Cluny

🎫 Moderate; free first Sun of every month

❓ Guided tours in English Sat–Sun (except first Sun of the month)

HIGHLIGHTS

- *Olympia*, Edouard Manet
- *Déjeuner sur l'Herbe*, Edouard Manet
- *Les Joueurs de Cartes*, Paul Cézanne
- ... es McNeill Whistler
- *L'Angélus*, Jean-François Millet
- *La Cathédrale de Rouen*, Claude Monet
- *Dans un Café*, Edgar Degas
- *La Chambre à Arles*, Vincent van Gogh
- *Femmes de Tahiti*, Paul Gauguin
- Chair by Charles Rennie Mackintosh

TIP

- A Paris Museum Pass (▷ 170) allows you to skip the lines for tickets.

You'll either love or hate the conversion of this 1900 train station. But whatever your view, its art collections, covering the years from 1848 to 1914, are a must for anyone interested in this crucial art period.

Monolithic When this museum finally opened in 1986 controversy ran high: Gae Aulenti's heavy stone structures lay unhappily under Laloux's delicate iron-and-glass shell, built as a train terminus in 1900. But the collections redeem this faux pas, offering a solid overview of the momentous period from Romanticism to Fauvism. Works by the giants of French art— Degas, Monet, Cézanne, Van Gogh, Renoir, Sisley and Pissarro—are the biggest crowd pullers. The opulent restaurant of the old Hôtel d'Orsay on the first floor is a historic monument.

Clockwise from far left: Check out the view through the giant clock in the museum's café; memories of a train station are evoked on the vast ground floor; the ornate station clock; the Musée d'Orsay sits elegantly beside the River Seine

Other highlights You can also see paintings that are examples of Naturalism, Symbolism and the Nabis school. There are sculptures by Rodin, Émile-Antoine Bourdelle and Aristide Maillol, and art nouveau furniture. Save time for the Salle des Fêtes (room 51), tucked away at the end of the middle level. The extravagantly chandeliered and mirrored room was originally part of the station's hotel.

Take a tour The chronological tour of the gallery starts with the Impressionists (including Manet, Degas, Monet, Renoir and Sisley) on Level 5, with Post-impressionists (including Van Gogh, Gauguin and Seurat) on the median level below, along with a sculpture gallery. A strong program of temporary exhibitions enhances the permanent collection.

THE BASICS

musee-orsay.fr

➕ F5

✉ 62 rue de Lille, 75007

☎ 01 40 49 48 14

🕐 Tue–Sun 9.30–6, Thu 9.30am–9.45pm

🍴 Restaurant on first floor; Café Campana and Café de l'Ours

Ⓜ Solférino

🚌 24, 63, 68, 69, 73, 83, 84, 94

🚊 RER Line C, Musée d'Orsay

♿ Excellent

💰 Moderate; free first Sun of every month

❓ Audio and guided tours, concerts and lectures

★13 Musée Picasso

HIGHLIGHTS

● Ceramics
● *Man with a Guitar*
● Studies for *Les Demoiselles d'Avignon*

TIP

● The museum works with other domestic and international cultural institutions, donating works for temporary exhibitions. As a result, gallery displays will change periodically.

Housing the largest collection of works by Picasso in the world, the Picasso Museum reopened with much aplomb in October 2014 after a $62-million face-lift, despite a budget overrun and political friction.

Taxes After Picasso died in 1973, his family owed about $50 million in death duties. In lieu of this they gave the state 203 of Picasso's paintings, 158 sculptures and many other items including curios he had collected and paintings by other artists. When his widow died in 1986, further works were handed over. The result was the basis of this remarkable collection covering all periods of the artist's life.

Hôtel Salé The building itself is a delight, originally built in the 1650s by a man who

Clockwise from far left: The elegant interior of the Musée Picasso; museum sign; ornate detail on the Hôtel Salé, a fitting home for the artist's works; the Hôtel Salé illuminated at night

gained his own wealth from collecting the very unpopular salt tax that was levied in France at the time. It later became an embassy, and a school, and was acquired by the French state in 1964. Four years later it was declared a historic monument, and it opened as the Musée Picasso in 1985.

The collection Spread over three floors, the collection does not contain the artist's best-known works, such as *Guernica*, but its delight is that it shows many works that he wanted to keep for himself. After all, he once declared himself the greatest collector of Picassos in the world, and here you will see examples of his work ranging from his Blue Period through to cubism, surrealism, which show the astonishing range of his talents.

THE BASICS

musee-picasso.fr

🔢 L5

✉ Hôtel Salé, 5 rue de Thorigny, 75003

☎ 01 85 56 00 36

🕐 Tue–Fri 11.30–6, Sat–Sun 9.30–6. Last admission 45 mins before closing.

🍴 Café

Ⓜ Saint-Paul, Saint-Sébastien–Froissart

♿ Very good

💰 Expensive

- A glass tower of 9,000 musical instruments
- Nepalese ritual lamp
- Aztec statues
- The Harter bequest of masks and sculptures from Cameroon

- The museum gardens are particularly magical in the evening, when they are beautifully illuminated.

This very eye-catching museum, near the Seine and Eiffel Tower, is dedicated to the cultural heritage of Africa, Asia, Oceania and the Americas.

A 21st-century venue Built on five levels and crowned by a wide terrace with fine views of the Eiffel Tower, the museum is hidden from view by trees and thick vegetation. *Le mur végétal* (plant wall) on the north facade is festooned with 15,000 plants representing 150 species from all over the world.

The collection A swooping white ramp leads through a dark tunnel to the display area, where you are greeted by a 10th-century anthropomorphic Dogon wood statue from Mali, its one remaining arm reaching skywards. This splendid

Clockwise from far left: Plants from all over the world cover the exterior of the museum; head of a figurine from Ifa, Nigeria, dating from the 12th to 14th century; Oceania Gallery; Uli wooden sculpture, 18th to early 19th century, from New Ireland, Oceania

beginning sets the tone for other highlights, including painted animal hides from the Americas, decorated with battle scenes and abstract earth and sky motifs; a glass tower of 9,000 musical instruments gathered from all corners of the world; and a headdress from Malekula Island, worn by dancers during rituals in the early 20th century. To aid navigation through the museum, each of the different regions has its own floor coloring.

Other attractions The museum stages several temporary exhibitions each year, as well as drama, dance and music in the theater. The museum organizes debates on historic and contemporary issues. Other attractions include a cinema, and regular hands-on workshops for adults and children from three years of age.

THE BASICS

quaibranly.fr

✚ B5

✉ 37 quai Branly, 75007 (also access via 218 rue de l'Université)

☎ 01 56 61 70 00

🕐 Sun, Tue–Wed 11–7, Thu–Sat 11–9

🍴 Les Ombres on the roof terrace (tel 01 47 53 68 00) and Café Branly in the garden

Ⓜ Alma–Marceau

🚌 42, 63, 72, 80, 92

🚆 RER Line C, Pont de l'Alma

♿ Good

💲 Moderate; gardens free

HIGHLIGHTS

- *Les Bourgeois de Calais (The Burghers of Calais)*
- *Le Penseur (The Thinker)*
- *La Porte de l'Enfer (The Gates of Hell)*
- *Le Baiser (The Kiss)*
- *La Main de Dieu (The Hand of God)*
- *Adam et Eve*
- *Ugolin*
- *Le Père Tanguy*, Van Gogh
- Original staircase

As an antidote to the military might of nearby Les Invalides (▷ 68–69) wander into the enchanting Musée Rodin, which unveiled the results of a renovation in 2015.

Hard times The rococo Hôtel Biron, which houses the museum, was built in 1730 and has an interesting history. One owner (the Duc de Lauzun) was sent to the guillotine and the house has been used successively as a dance hall, convent, school and artists' studios. Rodin lived here from 1908 until his death in 1917. In 1919 the house became a museum. The renovated chapel in the grounds is now used for temporary exhibitions.

Sculpture The elegant, luminous interior houses the collection that Rodin left to the

Clockwise from far left: The most famous Rodin sculpture, The Thinker, in the gardens; the facade of the museum; Rodin sculptures around the gardens; detail from The Burghers of Calais sculpture; the former Hôtel Biron, now housing the museum; more sculptures inside

nation. It ranges from his early sketches to the later watercolors and includes many of his most celebrated white marble and bronze sculptures, including *The Kiss* (*Le Baiser*). There are busts of the composer Mahler and writer Victor Hugo, among others, and a series of studies of Balzac. Alongside the Rodins are works by his contemporaries, in particular his tragic mistress and model, Camille Claudel, as well as Eugène Carrière, Edvard Munch, Renoir, Monet and Van Gogh. Rodin's furniture and antiques complete this exceptional collection.

Retreat The museum's private gardens cover 3ha (7.5 acres) and contain several major sculptures, a pond, flowering shrubs and benches for a quiet read. It's worth buying the garden-only ticket just for a respite from city life.

THE BASICS

musee-rodin.fr
✚ E6
✉ 79 rue de Varenne, 75007
☎ 01 44 18 61 10
🕐 Tue, Thu–Sun 10–5.45. Last admission 5.15. Wed 10–8.45. Last admission 8.15.
🍴 Peaceful garden café
Ⓜ Varenne, Invalides
🚌 69, 82, 87, 92
🚈 RER line C, Invalides
♿ Wheelchair access
🎫 Moderate; garden inexpensive

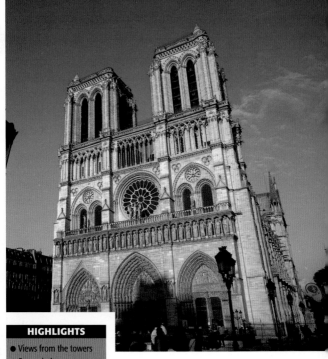

TIP

● Try to visit just before a service to experience the sense of anticipation as lights are turned on and people gather to worship.

Spectacular is the word to describe this extraordinary monument, with its 93m (305ft) spire and world-renowned flying buttresses. One of the finest views of the cathedral is from the *quais* to the east.

Evolution Construction of Notre-Dame started in 1163 and didn't finish until 1345. Since then the cathedral has suffered from pollution, politics, aesthetic trends and religious change. Most of the stained-glass windows were replaced with clear glass (the stained glass was later restored) in the 18th century, when Revolutionary zeal tore down statues and the spire was dismantled. Not least, Viollet-le-Duc, the fervent 19th-century medievalist architect, was let loose on its restoration and initiated radical alterations.

Clockwise from far left: The awe-inspiring Notre-Dame; soaring arches and rose windows in the nave; close-up of the flying buttresses and intricately carved Gothic tracery; stained-glass windows in the cathedral's Chapelle Saint-Georges; statue of the Virgin and Child

Interior grandeur The hushed, softly lit stone interior contains numerous chapels, tombs and statues. The sacristy on the south side of the choir is where the treasure of Notre-Dame is kept: medieval manuscripts, religious paraphernalia and relics, including the Crown of Thorns. Look at the magnificent stained glass above the mighty organ, one of the largest in Europe. The Crypt, often overlooked because its entrance is outside, contains Roman foundations and archaeological finds. Climb the towers (387 steps; no elevator) for fantastic views of the city and a close-up look at the stone gargoyles. Look at the three asymmetrical sculpted portals on the facade: These once served as a Bible for illiterate worshipers. Finally, walk round the outside of the cathedral for a view of its extravagant flying buttresses.

THE BASICS

notredamedeparis.fr
notre-dame-de-paris.
monuments-nationaux.fr
✚ J7
✉ Place du Parvis Notre-Dame–Place Jean-Paul II, 75004
☎ 01 42 34 56 10;
Crypt 01 55 42 50 10
🕐 Cathedral Mon–Fri 8–6.45, Sat–Sun 8–7.15. Towers Jul–Aug daily 10–6.30, until 11 Fri–Sat; Apr–Jun, Sep 10–6.30; Oct–Mar 10–5.30
🚇 Cité, Saint-Michel
🚌 21, 24, 38, 47, 85, 96
🚆 RER Lines B and C, Saint-Michel
♿ Good (not in towers)
🎫 Cathedral free; towers and Crypt moderate; treasury inexpensive

HIGHLIGHTS

- Grand Staircase
- Grand Foyer
- Auditorium
- Facade
- The shop, Galerie de l'Opéra de Paris (▷ 126)

This ornate wedding cake of a building, with sumptuous details decorating its every surface, presents the perfect epitaph to the frenetic architectural activities of France's Second Empire.

Past glory When Charles Garnier's opera house was inaugurated in 1875 it marked the end of Haussmann's ambitious urban face-lift and announced the cultural transition to the Belle Époque, with Nijinksy and Diaghilev's Ballets Russes as later highlights. The opera house, and a fatal accident with a chandelier in 1896, was the inspiration for the novel *The Phantom of the Opera* (1910) by Gaston Leroux. Today it stages both dance and opera. Rudolf Nureyev was director of the Paris Ballet here between 1983 and 1989.

From far left: The ornate facade of the Palais Garnier; one of Carrier-Belleuse's lamp-bearing statues; the gilded statue of Poetry on the roof of the building

Dazzle The Palais Garnier's extravagant, regilded facade of arches, winged horses, friezes, columns, lamps and much statuary, topped by a verdigris dome, leads into a majestic foyer. This is dominated by the Grand Staircase, dripping with balconies and chandeliers, which sweeps up to the Grand Foyer with its gilded mirrors, marble, murals and Murano glass. Don't miss the equally ornate auditorium, with its dazzling gold-leaf decorations and red-velvet seats, and Marc Chagall's incongruous and, at the time of its installation in 1964, controversial modernist ceiling whose naive scenes pay tribute to great opera and ballet and include recognizable Paris monuments. The auditorium can be visited except during rehearsals. The opera house also has a library and a museum of operatic memorabilia.

THE BASICS

operadeparis.fr

🚉 G3

✉ Place de l'Opéra, 75009

☎ 0892 89 90 90 (34¢ per minute)

🕐 Sep to mid-Jul 10–7; late Jul to Aug 10–6; ticket office Mon–Sat 11.30–6.30 (also one hour before performances)

🍴 Restaurant, bar

Ⓜ Opéra

🚌 20, 21, 22, 27, 29, 42, 52, 53, 66, 68, 81, 95

🚊 RER Line A, Auber

♿ Few; call for appointment, tel 01 40 01 18 50

💲 Moderate

❓ Guided tours in English (expensive, tel 0825 05 44 05); call for times

HIGHLIGHTS

- Oscar Wilde's tomb
- Edith Piaf's tomb
- Chopin's tomb
- Marcel Proust's tomb
- Mur des Fédérés
- Delacroix's tomb
- Baron Haussmann's tomb
- Molière's tomb
- Jim Morrison's tomb

If you think cemeteries are lugubrious then a visit here may change your mind. The plethora of tomb designs, trees and twisting paths create a peaceful setting.

Pilgrimage This landscaped hillside, east of the city center, is a popular haunt for rock fans, Piaf fans and lovers of poetry, literature, music and history. Since its creation in 1804 this vast cemetery has seen hundreds of famous people buried within its precincts, so that a walk around its labyrinthine expanse presents a microcosm of French socio-cultural history. Pick up a map at the entrance or plot your visit in advance on the website.

Incumbents The cemetery was created in 1804 on Jesuit land where Louis XIV's

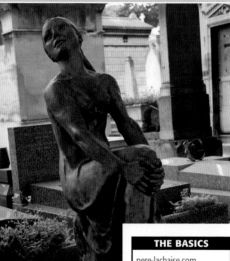

Clockwise from far left: Laid out in 1804 on the slopes of a hill in Ménilmontant, the cemetery is pleasantly shaded by trees; you can find peace and solitude at Père Lachaise; one of the many poignant statues; huge monuments line the wide avenues of the cemetery

confessor, Father La Chaise, once lived. It was the site of the Communards' tragic last stand in 1871, when the 147 survivors of a night-long fight met their bloody end in front of a government firing squad and were thrown into a communal grave, now commemorated by the Mur des Fédérés in the eastern corner. Memorials also commemorate victims of the Nazi concentration camps. Paths meander past striking funerary monuments and the graves of such well-known people as the star-crossed medieval lovers Abélard and Héloïse, painters Delacroix and Modigliani, actress Sarah Bernhardt, composers Poulenc and Bizet, and writers Balzac and Colette. Crowds of rock fans throng the tomb of Jim Morrison, singer with The Doors, who died in Paris in 1971.

THE BASICS

pere-lachaise.com
➕ See map ▷ 115
✉ Boulevard de Ménilmontant/rue du Repos, 75020
☎ 01 55 25 82 10
🕐 Mid-Mar to early Nov Mon–Fri 8–6, Sat 8.30–6, Sun 9–6; early Nov to mid-Mar Mon–Fri 8–5.30, Sat 8.30–5.30, Sun 9–5.30
🚇 Père Lachaise, Philippe Auguste, Gambetta
🚌 60, 64, 69
♿ Cobblestoned roads and hilly terrain
🎫 Free; tours moderate
❓ For information on guided tours in English visit parisinfo.com

HIGHLIGHTS

- Jeu de Paume
- Musée de l'Orangerie
- Hôtel de Crillon
- *Chevaux de Marly* (reproductions)
- View up the Champs-Élysées

As you stand in this noisy, traffic-choked square, it is hard to imagine the crowds baying for the deaths of Louis XVI and Marie-Antoinette, who were both guillotined here at the height of the French Revolution.

Gruesome history This pulsating square was initially laid out in the mid-18th century to accommodate a statue of King Louis XV. Under the new name of place de la Révolution, it then witnessed mass executions during the French Revolution and was finally renamed the place de la Concorde in 1795, as revolutionary zeal abated. In the same year, Guillaume Coustou's *Chevaux de Marly* were erected at the base of the Champs-Élysées (today reproductions; the originals are in the Louvre). Crowning the

Clockwise from far left: The ancient Egyptian obelisk takes pride of place; hieroglyphs on the obelisk; detail on a fountain; fountains play in elaborate splendor on the place de la Concorde; statues beneath the fountain; a diagram showing the erection of the obelisk

middle of the Concorde is a 3,000-year-old Egyptian obelisk overlooking eight symbolic statues of French cities. Use the pedestrian crossing to reach the central island for a closer look at the obelisk, framed by two fountains.

Grandeur To the north, on either side of the rue Royale, stand the colonnaded Hôtel de Crillon (on the left) and the matching Hôtel de la Marine (right), pre-Revolutionary relics. The rue Royale, with its luxury establishments, leads to the Madeleine. The eastern side of the Concorde is dominated by two public art galleries, both in the Jardin des Tuileries (▷ 24–25). The Jeu de Paume focuses on photography, while the beautifully renovated Orangerie (nearer the river) is famous for its panels of Monet's *Water Lilies* and Impressionist paintings.

THE BASICS

➕ E4–F4

✉ Place de la Concorde, 75008

☎ Jeu de Paume
01 47 03 12 50,
jeudepaume.org.
Musée de l'Orangerie
01 44 77 80 07,
musee-orangerie.fr

🕐 Jeu de Paume Tue
11–9, Wed–Sun 11–7.
Musée de l'Orangerie
Wed–Mon 9–6

🚇 Concorde

🚌 24, 42, 72, 73, 84, 94

♿ Jeu de Paume/
Musée de l'Orangerie
moderate

20 Place des Vosges

HIGHLIGHTS

- Pavillon du Roi
- Pavillon de la Reine
- Statue of Louis XIII
- No. 6, Maison de Victor Hugo
- No. 21, residence of Cardinal Richelieu
- Door knockers
- Trompe-l'œil bricks
- Four matching fountains

Paris's oldest and best-preserved square connects the quarters of the Marais and the Bastille. You can marvel at its architectural unity and stroll under the arcades, now animated by outdoor restaurants and window-shoppers.

Place Royale Ever since the square was inaugurated in 1612 with a spectacular fireworks display, countless luminaries have chosen to live in the redbrick houses overlooking the central garden of plane trees. Before that, the square was the site of a royal palace, the Hôtel des Tournelles (1388), which was later abandoned and demolished by Catherine de Médicis in 1559, when her husband Henri II died there. The arcaded facades were commissioned by Henri IV, who incorporated two royal

Clockwise from far left: The pristine place des Vosges; a refreshment break in the arcade; perfect architectural symmetry; even the road signs are attractive

pavilions at the heart of the north and south sides of the square and named it place Royale.

Exclusive address After the Revolution the square was renamed place des Vosges in tribute to the first French district to pay its new taxes. The first example of planned development the city, these 36 town houses (nine on each side and still intact), with their steep-pitched roofs, surround a formal garden laid out with gravel paths and fountains, all beautifully symmetrical. The square has attracted many famous residents, including princesses, official mistresses, Cardinal Richelieu, Victor Hugo (his house is now a museum) and Théophile Gautier. Smart shops and chic art galleries, with prices to match, line the square's arcades and are ideal for window-shopping.

THE BASICS

paris.fr
✚ M6
✉ Place des Vosges, 75004
🎫 Maison Victor Hugo Tue–Sun 10–6
🍴 Several
🚇 Bastille, Chemin Vert, Saint-Paul
🚌 20, 29, 76, 96
♿ Good
♨ Free

TIP

- Sacré-Cœur is a pleasant 10-minute walk from Abbesses or Anvers Métro. Or take the Montmartrobus from Abbesses to place du Tertre, from where it's a short walk.

Few people would admit it, but the high point of a trip here is not the basilica itself but the stunning views. You can't forget, however, that Sacré-Cœur was built in memory of the 58,000 dead of the Franco-Prussian War.

Perpetual prayer Although construction started in 1875, it wasn't until 1914 that this white neo-Romanesque-Byzantine edifice was completed, partly due to the problems of laying foundations in the quarry-riddled hill of Montmartre. Priests still work in relays to maintain the tradition of perpetual prayer for forgiveness for the horrors of war and atonement for those slaughtered during the Franco-Prussian war of 1870–71 and the massacre of some 20,000 Communards by

Clockwise from far left: Walking up to Sacré-Cœur; equestrian statue of Joan of Arc by Hippolyte Lefèbvre; mosaic of Christ in the basilica; one of the best views in Paris

government troops. The square bell tower was an afterthought and houses one of the world's heaviest bells, La Savoyarde, which weighs in at 19 tons. The stained-glass windows are replacements of those shattered by bombs in 1944.

Panoramas This unmistakable feature of the Paris skyline magnetizes the crowds arriving by funicular or via the steep steps of the terraced garden. For the best views, dawn and dusk offer particularly sparkling panoramas over the city, especially from the exterior terrace of the dome, the second-highest point in Paris after the Eiffel Tower. Just to the west of Sacré-Cœur is the diminutive Saint-Pierre, a much reworked though charming church, which is all that remains of the Benedictine abbey of Montmartre founded in 1133.

THE BASICS

sacre-coeur-montmartre.
com

🕂 c1

✉ Parvis du Sacré-Cœur, 75018

☎ 01 53 41 89 00

🕐 Daily 6am–10.30pm; dome and crypt 9.30–7 (6 in winter)

🚇 Abbesses (from here, walk along rue Yvonne Le Tac and rue Tardieu, then take funicular or walk up steps) or Anvers

🚌 Montmartrobus, 30, 31, 54, 67, 80, 85

♿ Wheelchair access from back of basilica

💶 Basilica and crypt free; dome moderate

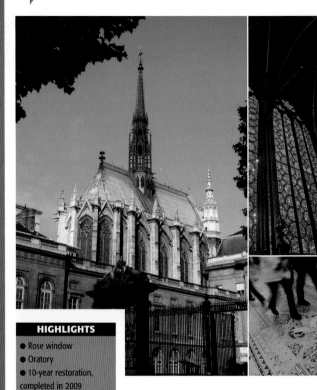

HIGHLIGHTS

● Rose window
● Oratory
● 10-year restoration, completed in 2009
● Tombs of canons
● Stained-glass depiction of Christ's Passion
● Saint Louis in the "Story of the Relics" window

TIPS

● The upper chapel can become extremely crowded. The quietest times to visit are Tuesday and Friday morning.
● Lines for tickets can be long so buy a ticket at La Conciergerie (▷ 18) if you want to save time.

Sainte-Chapelle's spire, towering 75m (246ft) above the ground, is in itself a great expression of faith, but this is surpassed inside by the glowing intensity of the stained-glass windows climbing to a star-studded roof, now spectacularly restored.

A masterpiece One of Paris's oldest and most significant monuments stands in the precincts of the Palais de Justice. The chapel was built by Louis IX (later canonized) to house the relics he had acquired at exorbitant cost during the crusades, including what was reputed to be the Crown of Thorns, as well as fragments of the Cross and drops of Christ's blood (now kept in Notre-Dame). Pierre de Montreuil is believed to have masterminded this delicate Gothic construction, bypassing the use of flying

Clockwise from far left: Sainte-Chapelle, with fine buttresses and a delicate spire; superb stained glass, depicting biblical scenes and featuring a rose window; intricate wood carving in the upper chapel; looking up at the magnificent ceiling; colorful wood carving; ornate patterned flooring

buttresses, incorporating a lower chapel for palace servants and installing more than 600 sq m (6,458 sq ft) of striking stained glass above. Completed in 1248 in record time, it was Louis IX's private chapel, with discreet access from what was then the royal palace.

Apocalypse More than 1,000 biblical scenes are illustrated in 15 windows, starting with Genesis to the left of the entrance, and working round the chapel to finish with the Apocalypse, in the rose window. The only non-biblical theme is in the 16th window, which tells how the holy relics came to Paris. Two-thirds of the windows are 13th-century originals—the oldest stained glass in Paris. The statues of the Apostles are copies; the originals are at the Musée National du Moyen-Âge (▷ 34–35).

THE BASICS

sainte-chapelle.monuments-nationaux.fr

✚ J6

✉ 4 boulevard du Palais, Île de la Cité, 75001

☎ 01 53 40 60 80

🕐 Mar–Oct daily 9.30–6; Nov–Feb 9–5

Ⓜ Cité, Châtelet

🚌 21, 24, 27, 38, 58, 70 85, 96

🚊 RER Line B, Saint-Michel

♿ Moderate (joint ticket expensive, ▷ panel 56)

❓ Guided tours in English; call for times

THE BOAT TRIP

Distance: 11km (7 miles)
Allow: Just over 1 hour
Start/End: Square du Vert-Galant, Pont Neuf
How to get there:
🚇 Pont Neuf
🚌 24, 27, 58, 67, 70, 72, 74, 75
From the Métro station, walk over the Pont Neuf. About halfway across, on the right, is a sign for the Vedettes du Pont Neuf. Go down the steps to the square.

TIPS

● Evening is a great time to go on this trip, when the monuments are lit up.
● A more flexible—though no cheaper—way to enjoy the river is the hop-on, hop-off Batobus shuttle service (▷ 167).

A pleasant river cruise along the Seine is a great way to view some of Paris's key sights from a different perspective. And in just over an hour you can see many of the famous landmarks.

Romantic trip The boat leaves from square du Vert-Galant and heads west. On the Right Bank you can see the Museé du Louvre (▷ 30–31). After passing under the Pont du Carrousel and the Pont Royal you'll see the Musée d'Orsay (▷ 36–37) on the Left Bank and then the 18th-century Palais Bourbon. On the Right Bank is place de la Concorde (▷ 50–51). The boat passes under the ornate Pont Alexandre III (▷ 73). On the Right Bank are the Grand Palais and Petit Palais (▷ 68) and on the Left Bank, in the distance, is Les Invalides (▷ 68–69). After

Clockwise from far left: View of Notre-Dame across the river; boats ply past the Eiffel Tower; a bateau-mouche trip along the Seine; boats at the Pont Neuf; a fine view of the Eiffel Tower and the footbridge, the Passerelle Debilly

passing under the Pont des Invalides, the Pont de l'Alma and the Passerelle Debilly, the boat rounds a bend to unveil a spectacular view of the Eiffel Tower (▷ 60–61) on the Left Bank. It then passes under the Pont d'Iéna, which spans the river between the Eiffel Tower and the Jardins du Trocadéro, before turning and heading back in the opposite direction to the Île de la Cité. You'll see the cupola of the Institut de France on the right before you pass under the southern side of the Pont Neuf. The next two bridges are the Pont Saint-Michel, leading to the Latin Quarter and the Sorbonne university, and the Petit Pont, the smallest bridge in Paris. On the Île de la Cité you can see Notre-Dame cathedral (▷ 44–45); the boat then circles the picturesque Île Saint-Louis before returning to the Pont Neuf past the Conciergerie.

THE BASICS

vedettesdupontneuf.com

☎ 01 46 33 98 38

🕐 Check online for sailing times

💷 Expensive

❓ Tours in English and French. Pick up a free route map from the boarding platform

HIGHLIGHTS

● Panoramic views
● Gustave Eiffel's office
● Sparkling lights

TIPS

● To skip the wait for the elevators, walk up the stairs to level two, then catch the elevator to the top. The climb isn't too daunting. Alternatively, buy your tickets online.
● The wait for the elevator is generally shorter at night.
● Strollers (buggies) are allowed up the tower only if they are collapsible.

The Eiffel Tower could be a cliché but it isn't. The powerful silhouette of Gustave Eiffel's marvel of engineering still makes a stirring sight, especially at night when its delicate, lace-like iron structure is accentuated by lights.

Glittering feat Built in a record two years for the 1889 Exposition Universelle, the Eiffel Tower was never intended to be a permanent feature of the city. However, in 1910 it was finally saved for posterity, preparing the way for today's 6.7 million annual visitors. Avoid a long wait for the elevator by visiting the tower at night, when it fully lives up to its romantic image and provides a glittering spectacle, whether of the illuminated tower itself or of the carpet of nocturnal Paris unfolding at its feet.

Clockwise from far left: The icon of Paris, set in the Champ de Mars; view of the tower from the Jardins du Trocadéro; the tower framed by the Wall of Peace; detail of the lace-like iron structure; the lower section dwarfs the crowds

More than 330 spotlights illuminate the lattice-work, topped by a rotating beacon. After dusk the tower sparkles for 5 minutes every hour on the hour until 1am, thanks to 20,000 randomly flashing low-energy bulbs.

Violent reactions Gustave Eiffel was a master of cast-iron structures; his prolific output included hundreds of factories, churches, via-ducts and bridges on four continents. His 324m (1,063ft) tower attracted great opposition, but his genius was vindicated by the fact that it sways no more than 9cm (3.5in) in high winds and remained the world's highest structure for 40 years. Eiffel kept an office here until his death in 1923; at the top, there is a re-creation of Thomas Edison's visit to the tower at the invitation of Eiffel on 10 September 1889.

THE BASICS

toureiffel.paris

🔼 B6

✉ Quai Branly, Champ de Mars, 75007

☎ 08 92 70 12 39

🕐 Sep to mid-Jun daily 9.30am–11.45pm; last elevator up at 10.30pm (stairs 9.30–6.30); mid-Jun to Aug 9am–12.45am; last elevator up at 11pm

🍴 Le 58 (1st floor, 08 25 56 66 62); Le Jules Verne (2nd floor, ▷ 149)

🚇 Bir-Hakeim, Trocadéro

🚌 42, 69, 82, 87

🚆 RER Line C, Tour Eiffel

♿ Very good (to 2nd floor). Wheelchair users are unable to go to the very top

💲 Expensive; 2nd stage moderate; stairs moderate

25 Versailles

HIGHLIGHTS

● Hall of Mirrors
● Petit Trianon
● Formal gardens
● Grandes Eaux
● Hameau and farm
● Buffet d'Eau, Grand Trianon
● Opera house

TIP

● Attend a performance to see the interior of the splendid 18th-century royal opera house.

The Château de Versailles has undergone a massive renovation that has restored much of the grandeur enjoyed by the Sun King, Louis XIV, who commissioned the palace.

A new palace Versailles is the ultimate symbol of French grandeur, and the backdrop to the death of the monarchy in 1789. Louis XIV moved his court to the site of his father's hunting lodge, creating a royal residence, seat of government and home to French nobility. Building continued until his death in 1715, by which time the 100ha (247-acre) garden had been perfected by landscape garden designer André Le Nôtre.

Glorious gardens With their geometric beds, vast watercourses and splendid fountains

Clockwise from far left: The magnificent château and the elaborate formal gardens; the lawns and lake with the Latona fountain in the foreground; the delightful floral fountain; ceiling detail in the Hall of Mirrors; the stunning Hall of Mirrors, the central feature of the château

THE BASICS

chateauversailles.fr

➕ See map ▷ 114

✉ Place d'Armes, Versailles 78000

☎ 01 30 83 78 00

🕐 State apartments Apr–Oct Tue–Sun 9–6.30; Nov–Mar Tue–Sun 9–5.30. Grand and Petit Trianon Tue–Sun 12–5.30 (until 6.30 in summer). Park daily 7am–8.30pm (8–6 in winter). Fountains Apr–Oct Sat–Sun 11–12, 3.30–5.30

🚉 RER C, Versailles Rive Gauche

♿ Few (State apartments)

💰 Passport ticket for all palaces expensive (visitors with disabilities free); park free; Grandes Eaux and Jardins Musicaux moderate Apr–Oct. (If you already have tickets, go to the A access. If not, go to the Ticket Information point, South Ministers' Wing.) Free first Sun of month Nov–Mar

❓ Guided tours

(flowing weekends Apr–Oct), the palace gardens are the perfect expression of the formal French style. Geometry rules, too, in the floral gardens at the lavish royal retreat of Grand Trianon, but Marie-Antoinette's romantic estate at the Petit Trianon is informal and pretty. It comprises a small château, belvedere, rustic hamlet (Hameau de la Reine) and the notorious but delightful farm where the queen liked to play at being a milkmaid.

Architectural highlights The magnificence of the Hall of Mirrors is the highlight of the Grands Appartements, where you can also access the opulent Queen's Chamber (closed for renovation from January 2016). At weekends, you can visit the more intimate apartments of the Dauphin and Louis XV's daughters.

More to See

This section contains other great places to visit if you have more time. Some are in the heart of the city while others are a short journey away, found under Farther Afield. This chapter also has fantastic excursions that you should set aside a whole day to visit.

MORE TO SEE

In the Heart of the City

CAFÉ BEAUBOURG

cafebeaubourg.com

Opposite the Pompidou Centre, this café is frequented by artists, critics and book-reading poseurs.

🞤 K5 ✉ 43 rue Saint-Merri, 75004 ☎ 01 48 87 63 96 🕐 Daily 8am–2am. Last orders midnight 🚇 Hôtel de Ville, Châtelet, Rambuteau

CAFÉ LES DEUX MAGOTS

lesdeuxmagots.fr

This famous Left Bank café welcomes a mix of tourists and those following in the footsteps of Albert Camus and Ernest Hemingway.

🞤 G6 ✉ 6 place Saint-Germain-des-Prés, 75006 ☎ 01 45 48 55 25 🕐 Daily 7.30am–1am 🚇 Saint-Germain-des-Prés

CAFÉ DE FLORE

Haunted by ghosts of existentialists Sartre and de Beauvoir, who held court here during the Occupation, this café is pricey but a good spot for people-watching over a cup of hot chocolate.

🞤 G6 ✉ 172 boulevard Saint-Germain, 75006 ☎ 01 45 48 55 26 🕐 Daily 7am–2am 🚇 Saint-Germain-des-Prés

CIMETIÈRE DE MONTMARTRE

Montmartre's cemetery is packed with graves of the famous, including composers Hector Berlioz and Jacques Offenbach, writers Henri Stendhal and Alexandre Dumas, artists Edgar Degas and Jean-Baptiste Greuze, and singer Dalida. The imposing tomb of Émile Zola is close to the flower-filled roundabout near the main entrance, although the writer's remains were moved to the Panthéon in 1908.

🞤 a1 ✉ 20 avenue Rachel, 75018 ☎ 01 53 42 36 30 🕐 Mid-Mar to early Nov Mon–Sat 8.30–6, Sun 9–6; Nov to mid-Mar Mon–Sat 8.30–5.30, Sun 9–5.30. Last entry 15 mins before closing 🚇 Place de Clichy, Blanche

DOMAINE NATIONAL DU PALAIS ROYAL

palais.royal.monuments-nationaux.fr

Elegant 18th-century shopping arcades surround this garden and palace (now the Conseil Constitutionnel and the Ministère de la Culture). Daniel Buren's striking striped columns occupy the Cour d'Honneur.

Outside Café les Deux Magots

Monument at the Cimetière de Montmartre

➕ H4 ✉ Place du Palais-Royal, 75001
☎ 01 47 03 92 16 🕐 Apr–May daily 7am–
10.15pm; Jun–Aug 7am–11pm; Sep
7am–9.30pm; Oct–Mar 7am–8.30pm
🍽 Plenty 🚇 Palais-Royal–Musée du Louvre

DROUOT RICHELIEU
drouot.com
Paris's main auction rooms are
where anything from a Persian
carpet to a Louis XV commode
may come under the hammer.
➕ H2 ✉ 9 rue Drouot, 75009 ☎ 01 48
00 20 20 🕐 Mon–Sat 11–6 (most auctions
start at 2pm); closed Aug 🚇 Richelieu–
Drouot

ÉGLISE SAINT-ÉTIENNE-DU-MONT
saintetiennedumont.fr
Dating from the 15th century, this
church has a bizarre combination
of Gothic, Renaissance and classical architecture. The unique screen
arching over the nave is a highlight.
➕ J8 ✉ Place Sainte-Geneviève, 75005
☎ 01 43 54 11 79 🕐 Tue–Fri 8–7.45, Sat
8.45–12, 2–7.45, Sun 8.45–12.15, 2–7.45
(hours can vary during holidays)
🚇 Cardinal Lemoine

ÉGLISE SAINT-EUSTACHE
saint-eustache.org
Renaissance in detail and decoration but Gothic in general design,
this church has frequent concerts.
➕ J4 ✉ 2 impasse Saint-Eustache, 75001
☎ 01 42 36 31 05 🕐 Mon–Fri 9.30–7,
Sat–Sun 9–7 🚇 Les Halles

ÉGLISE SAINT-GERMAIN-DES-PRÉS
eglise-sgp.org
Paris's oldest church dates from
the 11th century and preserves an
original tower and choir. There are
organ and concert recitals.
➕ G6 ✉ Place Saint-Germain-des-Prés,
75006 ☎ 01 55 42 81 10 🕐 Daily 8–7.45
🚇 Saint-Germain-des-Prés

ÉGLISE SAINT-MERRI
saintmerry.org
This superb example of Flamboyant
Gothic, not completed until 1612,
has Renaissance stained glass,
murals and an impressive organ
loft. It also holds concerts.
➕ K5 ✉ 76 rue de la Verrerie, 75004
☎ 01 42 71 53 33. See accueilmusical.fr for
concert information 🚇 Hôtel de Ville

Église Saint-Eustache

Église Saint-Germain-des-Prés

ÉGLISE SAINT-SÉVERIN

saint-severin.com

Built between the 13th and 16th centuries on the site of an 11th-century church, the interior features lovely stained glass and palm-tree vaulting.

🔲 J7 ✉ 3 rue des Prêtres Saint-Séverin, 75005 ☎ 01 42 34 93 50 🕐 Mon–Sat 11–7.30, Sun 9–8.30 🚇 Saint-Michel, Cluny–La Sorbonne

ÉGLISE SAINT-SULPICE

pss75.fr

Work started here in 1646, ending 134 years later with asymmetrical towers and mixed styles. Note Delacroix's murals in the first chapel on the right and 18th-century wood paneling in the sacristy.

🔲 G7 ✉ Place Saint-Sulpice, 75006 ☎ 01 42 34 59 98 🕐 Daily 7.30–7.30 🚇 Saint-Sulpice

GRAND PALAIS AND PETIT PALAIS

grandpalais.fr.
petitpalais.paris.fr

These two fine buildings were erected for the Universal Exposition of 1900 in the fashionable beaux-arts style. Today they perform an important arts function. The Petit Palais houses a permanent collection as the Musée des Beaux-Arts with pieces from the Classical era to the early 20th century. The Grand Palais lends its immense space to an eclectic program of traveling exhibitions.

🔲 D4/E4 ✉ Grand Palais: avenue du General Eisenhower. Petit Palais: avenue Winston Churchill ☎ Grand Palais: 01 44 13 17 17. Petit Palais: 01 53 43 40 00 🚇 Champs-Élysées–Clemenceau

ÎLE SAINT-LOUIS

An oasis of calm, the Île Saint-Louis maintains a spirit of its own. Rue Saint-Louis-en-l'Île is lined with art shops and restaurants.

🔲 K/L7 🚇 Pont Marie, Sully Morland

INSTITUT DU MONDE ARABE

imarabe.org

The high-tech reinterpretation of traditional Arab fretwork is the hallmark here. The museum has fine metalwork, ceramics, textiles, carpets and calligraphy.

Vaulted ceiling, Gothic arches and stained glass inside Église Saint-Séverin

🚇 K7 ✉ 1 rue des Fossés Saint-Bernard, 75005 ☎ 01 40 51 38 38 🕐 Tue–Thu 10–6, Fri 10–9.30, Sat–Sun 10–7 🚇 Cardinal Lemoine, Jussieu 💶 Moderate

LES INVALIDES

musee-armee.fr

Les Invalides was built to house invalid soldiers and this tradition continues today. The greatest figures of French military history, most notably Napoleon himself, are interred in the Église du Dôme, while their battles are illustrated in the Musée de l'Armée, to be found on the same site.

🚇 D6 ✉ 129 rue de Grenelle, 75007 ☎ 08 10 11 33 99 🕐 Apr–Oct daily 10–6; Nov–Mar 10–5. Last admission 30 mins before closing. Closed first Mon of month (except Jul–Sep). Église du Dôme until 7pm Jul–Aug 🚇 La Tour Maubourg, École Militaire, Varenne 💶 Moderate

MAISON EUROPÉENNE DE LA PHOTOGRAPHIE

mep-fr.org

This is a stylish complex for contemporary photography, with dynamic temporary shows. The galleries are spread over five floors of the 18th-century Hôtel Hénault de Cantobre and a new wing.

🚇 L6 ✉ 5–7 rue de Fourcy, 75004 ☎ 01 44 78 75 00 🕐 Wed–Sun 11am–7.45pm 🚇 Saint-Paul 💶 Moderate

MÉMORIAL DE LA SHOAH

memorialdelashoah.org

This moving Holocaust museum contains a wall inscribed with the names of the 76,000 Jewish people deported from France between 1942 and 1944. It also mounts temporary exhibitions on Holocaust-related themes.

🚇 K6 ✉ 17 rue Geoffroy-l'Asnier, 75004 ☎ 01 42 77 44 72 🕐 Sun–Fri 10–6 (Thu until 10) 🚇 Saint-Paul, Hôtel de Ville, Pont Marie 💶 Free

MUSÉE D'ART ET D'HISTOIRE DU JUDAÏSME

mahj.org

Jewish art and culture are on display here, from medieval times to the present day, concentrating mainly on France but also including the rest of Europe and North Africa. Exhibits range from wedding

A sign at the Maison Européenne de la Photographie

The formal gardens in front of Les Invalides

MORE TO SEE

items, *objets d'art*, manuscripts and textiles to works by Jewish artists such as Modigliani and Chagall.
➕ K5 ✉ Hôtel de Saint-Aignan, 71 rue du Temple, 75003 ☎ 01 53 01 86 60 🕐 Mon–Fri 11–6, Sun 10–6. Last admission 45 mins before closing 🚇 Rambuteau, Hôtel de Ville 💷 Moderate

MUSÉE D'ART MODERNE DE LA VILLE DE PARIS
mam.paris.fr
Outstanding temporary exhibitions have earned this modern-art museum an international reputation. The collection covers fauvism, cubism, surrealism, abstract and Nouveau Réalisme. *La Danse* (1931–33), a mural by Henri Matisse, hangs in a room devoted to the artist. The museum occupies the east wing of the Palais de Tokyo; the west wing houses the Centre d'Art Contemporain.
➕ B4 ✉ 11 avenue du Président Wilson, 75016 ☎ 01 53 67 40 00 🕐 Tue–Wed, Fri–Sun 10–6, Thu 10–10. Last admission 45 mins before closing 🚇 léna, Alma–Marceau 💷 Free; temporary exhibitions moderate

MUSÉE DES ARTS DÉCORATIFS
lesartsdecoratifs.fr
This collection of decorative arts is enriched by contributions from 20th-century designers such as Le Corbusier, Mallet-Stevens, Niki de Saint Phalle and Philippe Starck. Another branch of the museum is the Musée Nissim Camondo on rue de Monceau, an early 20th century-mansion complete with original decor.
➕ G5 ✉ 107 rue de Rivoli, 75001 ☎ 01 44 55 57 50 🕐 Tue–Sun 11–6 (Thu until 9). Last admission 30 mins before closing 🚇 Palais-Royal–Musée du Louvre 💷 Moderate; combined ticket for all sites expensive

MUSÉE DES ARTS ET MÉTIERS
arts-et-metiers.net
Art meets science at this museum through antique clocks, optics, underwater items including a diving suit, vintage cars and mechanical toys.
➕ K4 ✉ 60 rue Réaumur, 75003 ☎ 01 53 01 82 00 🕐 Tue–Sun 10–6 (Thu until 9.30pm) 🚇 Arts et Métiers, Réaumur–Sébastopol 💷 Moderate

Musée d'Art Moderne de la Ville de Paris

Modern design at the Musée des Arts Décoratifs

MUSÉE COGNACQ-JAY

museecogancqjay.paris.fr

In a magnificent Marais mansion furnished in 18th-century style, you can see the 18th-century paintings and *objets d'art* collected by Ernest Cognacq and his wife Louise Jay, founders of the La Samaritaine department store.

➕ L6 ✉ Hôtel Donon, 8 rue Elzévir, 75003 ☎ 01 40 27 07 21 🕐 Tue–Sun 10–6 🚇 Saint-Paul 🎫 Free

MUSÉE GUSTAVE MOREAU

musee-moreau.fr

This studio-museum, on the edge of Pigalle, presents an intriguing view of how a late-19th-century artist lived and worked. On the second and third floors are the studios of the symbolist painter Gustave Moreau (1826–98), teacher to Henri Matisse; on the first floor is a reconstruction of Moreau's private apartment.

➕ G2 ✉ 14 rue de la Rochefoucauld, 75009 ☎ 01 48 74 38 50 🕐 Mon, Wed, Thu 10–12.45, 2–5.15, Fri–Sun 10–5.15 🚇 Trinité 🎫 Moderate; free first Sun of the month

MUSÉE JACQUEMART-ANDRÉ

musee-jacquemart-andre.com

This elegant mansion was built between 1869 and 1876 for the Parisian financier Eduard André and his wife, the artist Nélie Jacquemart. It is filled with original furniture and a fine collection of paintings, including works by Botticelli, Rembrandt, Bellini, Van Dyck, Fragonard and Jacques-Louis David.

➕ D2 ✉ 158 boulevard Haussmann, 75008 ☎ 01 45 62 11 59 🕐 Daily 10–6 🚇 Saint-Philippe-du-Roule, Miromesnil 🎫 Moderate (audio guide included)

MUSÉE DE MONTMARTRE

museedemontmartre.fr

Montmartre's intriguing history includes a headless saint, prosperous windmills and a notoriously liberal nightlife. You can find out more at the unassuming Musée de Montmartre at the renovated studio of mother and son artists Suzanne Valadon and Maurice Utrillo.

➕ c1 ✉ 12 rue Cortot, 75018 ☎ 01 49 25 89 39 🕐 Daily 10–6 🚇 Lamarck Caulaincourt, Anvers 🎫 Moderate

Paintings at the Musée Gustave Moreau

Facade of the Musée Gustave Moreau

MUSÉUM NATIONAL D'HISTOIRE NATURELLE, JARDIN DES PLANTES

mnhn.fr

Set up in 1635 on the initiative of Louis XIII's physician, the Jardin des Plantes is Paris's botanical garden, complete with an alpine section and hothouses. Ranged around its fringes are the buildings of the Muséum National d'Histoire Naturelle, of which the garden forms part. These include the Galeries d'Anatomie Comparée et de Paléontologie, housing dinosaur skeletons, and the Grande Galerie de l'Évolution with a children's gallery devoted to biodiversity.

➕ K9–L8/9 ✉ 2 rue Buffon, 75005
☎ 01 40 79 54 79 ⏰ Apr–Sep Mon, Wed, Sat–Sun 10–6; Oct–Mar Wed–Mon 10–5 🚇 Gare d'Austerlitz, Jussieu 💷 Jardin free, others moderate

PALAIS DE CHAILLOT

Built for the Paris exhibition of 1937, the curving wings of the Palais de Chaillot house the Musée de la Marine, the Musée de l'Homme, the Cité de l'Architecture et du Patrimoine and the Théatre de Chaillot. The wide terraced Parvis des Libertés et des Droits de l'Homme, between the two wings, offers fabulous views of the city.

➕ A5 ✉ Place du Trocadéro, 75116
☎ Marine 01 35 65 69 69, musee-marine.fr. Homme 01 44 05 72 72, museedelhomme. fr 🚇 Trocadéro 💷 Moderate

PANTHÉON

pantheon.monuments-nationaux.fr

Occupying a hilltop site close to the Sorbonne and the Quartier Latin, Soufflot's cathedral-like neo-classical 18th-century structure provides an imposing setting for the tombs of France's greatest citizens, including Voltaire, Dumas, Rousseau and Marie Curie. From April to October, you can ascend the dome as part of a guided tour.

➕ J8 ✉ Place du Panthéon, 75005
☎ 01 44 32 18 00 ⏰ Apr–Sep daily 10–6.30; Oct–Mar 10–6 🚇 Cardinal Lemoine, Maubert–Mutualité 💷 Moderate

PARC DU CHAMP DE MARS

The lawns of the Champ de Mars stretch out in a rectangular design

Aerial view of the Champ de Mars from the Eiffel Tower

between the Eiffel Tower and the 18th-century École Militaire. The Romans fought the Celtic Parisii tribe here in 52BC—the park's name, Field of Mars, refers to the Roman god of war. It wasn't until 1765 that the site became a parade ground for the École Militaire. The park has hosted national celebrations, parades, international exhibitions and horse races. Today it is popular with families, joggers and visitors.

🔹 B6–C6 ✉ Champ de Mars, 75007
🚇 École Militaire

PAVILLON DE L'ARSENAL

pavillon-arsenal.com
This strikingly designed building houses well-conceived exhibitions on urban Paris past and present, alongside a display on the city's architectural evolution.

🔹 L7 ✉ 21 boulevard Morland, 75004
☎ 01 42 76 33 97 🕐 Tue–Sat 10.30–6.30, Sun 11–7 🚇 Sully Morland 🎟 Free

PLACE DES ABBESSES

Place des Abbesses is less touristy than place du Tertre, farther up the Montmartre hill, so it's a quieter coffee stop. The magnificent art nouveau Métro entrance here leads into Paris's deepest station, 30m (98.5ft) below ground. It was designed by Hector Guimard (1867–1942) and is one of only three original Guimard entrances left in Paris. The church of Saint-Jean-de-Montmartre (1904) picks up on the art nouveau theme, with decorative windows enlivening the rather ugly redbrick cladding.

🔹 C2 ✉ Place des Abbesses, Montmartre, 75018 🚇 Abbesses

PONT ALEXANDRE III

Four gilded bronze Pegasus figures watch over this wildly ornate bridge, which forms a link between Les Invalides (▷ 69) on the Left Bank and the Grand Palais and Petit Palais (▷ 68) on the Right. Symbolic of the optimism of the Belle Époque, it was built for the 1900 Exposition Universelle. The bridge is crammed with elaborate decoration by more than 15 artists.

🔹 D4 ✉ Cours de la Reine/quai d'Orsay
🚇 Invalides, Champs-Élysées–Clémenceau

Art nouveau entrance to the Abbesses Métro station, designed by Hector Guimard

Bronze figures on the Pont Alexandre III

PONT DE L'ALMA

The first Pont de l'Alma was built in 1856 to commemorate a victory over the Russians by the Franco-British alliance in the Crimean War. The bridge was replaced in 1974. The underpass on the Right Bank is where the fatal car crash involving Diana, Princess of Wales, occurred in August 1997. The Liberty Flame near the entrance, a symbol of American and French friendship, has become an unofficial memorial.

🞦 C4/C5 ⊠ Place de l'Alma/place de la Résistance 🚇 Alma–Marceau

PONT DES ARTS

The pedestrian bridge of 1804 was replaced in 1984 by an iron structure of seven arches crossed by wooden planks. From the center of the bridge there are excellent views of the Seine. This is a popular spot for lovers to stroll.

🞦 H5–6 🚇 Louvre–Rivoli

PONT DE BIR-HAKEIM

Built between 1903 and 1905, the two-tier art nouveau structure has a walkway, roadway and a Métro viaduct. It is made up of two unequal metal structures on either side of the allée des Cygnes. The bridge was given its name in 1949, in memory of the victory of General Koenig in Libya in 1942.

🞦 A6 ⊠ Quai Branly/avenue du Président Kennedy 🚇 Bir-Hakeim, Passy

PONT NEUF

Dating from 1604, Paris's oldest bridge ironically bears the name of New Bridge. The houseless design was highly controversial at the time.

🞦 H6 🚇 Pont Neuf, Île de la Cité

RUE DU CHERCHE-MIDI

César's sculpture on the rue de Sèvres crossroads marks out this typical Left Bank street, home to the famous Poîlane bakery (No. 8) and the Musée Hébert (No. 85).

🞦 G7 🚇 Saint-Sulpice

RUE DU FAUBOURG SAINT-HONORÉ

Price tags and politics cohabit in this street of luxury. Admire Hermès' imaginative window

Pont de Bir-Hakeim

Houses behind the Pont Neuf

dressing or salute the gendarmes in front of the Élysée Palace.

➕ E3 🚇 Madeleine, Miromesnil

RUE JACOB

Antiques and interior decoration shops monopolize this picturesque stretch. You can detour to the nearby Musée National Eugène Delacroix on rue de Furstenberg.

➕ G6 🚇 Saint-Germain-des-Prés

RUE DES ROSIERS

At the heart of Paris's lively Jewish quarter, this effervescent street is packed with synagogues, kosher butchers and restaurants, and Hebrew bookshops as well as an array of designer boutiques.

➕ L6 🚇 Saint-Paul

RUE VIEILLE-DU-TEMPLE

The pulse of the hip Marais district, this street is dense with bars, cafés, restaurants and boutiques.

➕ K6–L5 🚇 Saint-Paul

SQUARE DU VERT-GALANT

Enjoy a quintessential view of the picturesque bridges and the iconic Louvre in this tiny, pretty park, which is also the perfect place for a picnic.

➕ H6 ✉ Place du Pont-Neuf, 75001 🚇 Pont Neuf

TOUR MONTPARNASSE

tourmontparnasse56.com

When it was constructed in 1973, with its reinforced concrete core, the Tour Montparnasse's 59 floors of smoked glass provoked some indignation. Since then it has become a familiar landmark, visible from all over Paris, and is spectacular by night when the hundreds of windows light up the sky. The 56th-floor viewing gallery and the 59th-floor terrace of this 210m (688ft) tower offer fine views of the city. On a clear day you can see up to 40km (25 miles). Films on Paris (in French) are screened on the 56th floor.

➕ F9 ✉ 33 avenue du Maine, 75015 ☎ 01 45 38 52 56 🕐 Apr–Sep daily 9.30am–11.30pm; Oct–Mar 9.30am–10.30pm (until 11 Fri–Sat). Last elevator up 30 mins before closing 🚇 Montparnasse–Bienvenüe 💶 Expensive

Buildings reflected in a Lanvin shop window at rue du Faubourg Saint-Honoré

Square du Vert-Galant

Farther Afield

FONDATION LOUIS VUITTON

fondationlouisvuitton.fr

The city's newest museum, with its futuristic edifice designed by Frank Gehry, opened in 2014. It showcases the art collections of the Louis Vuitton French haute-couture house and temporary exhibitions.

➕ See map ▷ 114 ✉ 8 avenue du Mahatma Gandhi, Bois de Boulogne 75116 ☎ 01 40 69 96 00 🕐 Mon, Wed–Thu 12–7, Fri 12–11, Sat–Sun 10–8 (closed Tue); during French school holidays Sat–Thu (including Tue) 10–8, Fri 10–11 🚇 Les Sablons; minibus from place Charles de Gaulle every 15 mins (ticket €1) 💷 Expensive

LA GRANDE ARCHE

grandearche.com

This modernist echo of the Arc de Triomphe in white marble and on a grand scale was designed by Johann Otto von Spreckelsen. On the rooftop is a Computer Museum.

➕ See map ▷ 114 ✉ 1 parvis de La Défense, 92044 ☎ 01 49 07 27 27 🕐 Apr–Aug daily 10–8; Sep–Mar 10–7 🚇 Grande Arche de La Défense 💷 Moderate

La Grande Arche in La Défense

PARC ANDRÉ-CITROËN

This futurist 1990s park divided into specialist gardens lies on the site of a former Citroën factory. You'll find zany experimentation with metal and water, plus a tethered balloon.

➕ See map ▷ 114 ✉ Rue Cauchy, 75015 🕐 Summer daily 8–dusk (9–dusk rest of year) 🚇 Balard, Javel 💷 Free

PARC DES BUTTES CHAUMONT

The loveliest of Haussmann's parks owes its singular beauty and fine views to its craggy site, a former quarry in the northeast of the city. There is also a children's puppet theater, the Guignol de Paris.

➕ See map ▷ 115 ✉ 1 rue Botzaris, 75019 🕐 May to mid-Sep daily 7am–10pm; mid-Sep 7am–9pm; Oct–Apr 7am–8pm 🚇 Buttes Chaumont 💷 Free

PARC DE LA VILLETTE

lavillette.com

The Parc de la Villette catapults you into a futuristic world. It offers cultural attractions and leisure activities including a science museum, music complex, hemispheric cinema, exhibition venue and the city's flagship concert hall, the Philharmonie de Paris, designed by Jean Nouvel and opened in 2015. A covered walkway runs the length of the park, linking the Cité des Sciences et de l'Industrie and the Cité de la Musique.

➕ See map ▷ 115 ✉ Park 211 avenue Jean-Jaurès 75019 ☎ Park 01 40 03 75 75. Cité de Sciences et de l'Industrie 01 40 04 80 00. Cité de la Musique 01 44 84 44 84 🕐 Cité des Sciences et de l'Industrie Tue–Sat 10–6, Sun 10–7. Cité de la Musique Tue–Sat 12–6, Sun 10–6 🍴 Cafés, restaurants 🚇 Park: Porte de Pantin. Cité des Sciences et de l'Industrie. Porte de la Villette 💷 Park: free; Cité des Sciences et de l'Industrie: expensive ❓ Reserve activities as soon as you arrive

Excursions

CHANTILLY

domainedechantilly.com

Picturesque Château de Chantilly is surrounded by attractive parkland, with the forest of Chantilly beyond, and contains a magnificent art collection. The town of Chantilly is one of Europe's leading training venues for racehorses and is home to a world-famous racecourse and the Musée du Cheval, housed in the Grandes Écuries—a superb 18th-century stable block.

For five centuries, the domain of Chantilly passed from one branch of the same family to another without ever being sold, starting with the Orgemont family in the 14th and 15th centuries before passing to the Montmorencys, one of the most powerful families in the kingdom. Chantilly passed in turn to the Bourbon Condés, cousins of the kings of France.

The old château was ruined during the Revolution, but in the late 19th century a splendid reconstruction was commissioned by Henri d'Orléans, duc d'Aumale, the son of King Louis Philippe, who needed somewhere to house his art collection. It is still hung in the Galerie des Peintures in the manner stipulated by him when he bequeathed Chantilly to the nation. The collection includes works by Raphael and Botticelli, Watteau, Delacroix and Ingres. The château opened as a museum in 1898, a year after the duke's death. The Grands Appartements are in the Renaissance wing of the Petit Château adjacent to the main building, and include the charming Grande Singerie, an 18th-century boudoir decorated with images of monkeys and chinoiserie.

Distance: 48km (30 miles)

Journey Time: 24 mins (SNCF train)/ 45 mins (RER train)

✉ Chantilly 60500 ☎ 03 44 27 31 80 🕐 Château Apr–Oct daily 10–6; Nov–Mar 10.30–5. Closed early–late Jan. Grand Stables and Musée du Cheval same as Château 🚉 Chantilly-Gouvieux SNCF, RER line D; free bus from station to château 🚌 PARISCityVISION runs day tours by coach, departing from rue des Pyramides, 75001 (tel 01 44 55 60 00, pariscityvision. com) 💷 Expensive

The delightful Château de Chantilly

A winged statue in the Temple of Love, in the grounds of the Château de Chantilly

DISNEYLAND® PARIS

disneylandparis.com

Disneyland® Paris attracts millions of visitors to its two Parks—Disneyland® Park and Walt Disney Studios® Park. The resort, in the Marne-la-Vallée countryside east of Paris, opened in 1992. The Walt Disney Studios® Park was added in 2002. Other attractions include the Disney Village entertainment complex, seven hotels and even a golf course.

Disneyland® Paris offers the traditional Disney experience with family-friendly attractions such as Main Street USA, with its recreation of small town America in the early 20th century, including an old-fashioned steam train and horse-drawn streetcars. There are rides to suit all ages and levels of bravery, from the charming musical journey of "it's a small world" to the lavish Pirates of the Caribbean ride and Buzz Lightyear Laser Blast—a laser shoot-out. White-knuckle rides include Space Mountain®: Mission 2 and Big Thunder Mountain, a journey on a runaway mine train. Minimum height and age restrictions apply on some rides.

Walt Disney Studios® Park's scarier rides include the terrifying Twilight Zone Tower of Terror™—an abandoned art deco hotel in which the elevator drops at faster than the speed of gravity—and the Rock 'n' Roller Coaster starring Aerosmith, a fast, looping roller coaster that accelerates from 0 to 100kph (62mph) in just three seconds.

Much of what there is to see in Walt Disney Studios® Park is specifically film-related and includes the extraordinary stunt driving of Moteurs...Action! Stunt Show Spectacular and the animation-themed attractions of Toon Studio. At Art of Disney Animation® you'll learn the techniques used to animate a Disney cartoon before getting the opportunity to try it for yourself.

Distance: 44km (27 miles)

Journey Time: 35 mins

✉ Marne-la-Vallée, 77777, Cedex 4

☎ 0825 300 500 🚇 RER Line A, Marne-la-Vallée 💶 Expensive

Sleeping Beauty Castle, Disneyland® Paris

Space Mountain®: Mission 2, Disneyland® Paris

FONTAINEBLEAU

musee-chateau-fontainebleau.fr

Fontainebleau has witnessed momentous events, including the birth of Louis XIII in 1601 and Napoleon signing his deed of abdication in 1814. Kings went hunting in the forest here as far back as the 12th century.

With more than 1,500 rooms and 53ha (130 acres) of parkland, the royal château of Fontainebleau is, despite its associations with *la chasse*, no mere hunting lodge. What sets it apart is that it was the only royal and imperial residence in France to be inhabited continuously for seven centuries, and is consequently a showcase for French architecture in the grand style. The surviving medieval keep forms the core of the building, which was subsequently extended in splendid Renaissance style under François I and, in the 17th century, during the reign of Henri IV. A further wing was built during the time of Louis XV; after the Revolution, the château was restored by Napoleon Bonaparte. Its final royal inhabitant was Napoleon III, whose court stayed here until 1869.

The most spectacular of the interiors are the Renaissance rooms, inspired by the new artistic styles François I had seen in Italy. These rooms include the sumptuous ballroom and François I's magnificent long gallery. Altogether more intimate in scale are Marie Antoinette's boudoirs and the apartment of Louis XIV's secret second wife, Madame de Maintenon. Outside, the Grand Parterre is reputedly the largest formal garden in Europe.

Distance: 68km (42 miles)
Journey Time: 50 mins

☎ 01 60 71 50 70 🕒 Château Apr–Sep Wed–Mon 9.30–6; Oct–Mar Wed–Mon 9.30–5. Last admission 45 mins before closing. Courtyard and gardens May–Sep daily 9–7; Mar–Apr, Oct 9–6; Nov–Feb 9–5. Park daily 24 hours 🚉 Fontainebleau–Avon 🚌 PARISCityVISION runs half-day and day tours by coach, departing from rue des Pyramides, 75001 (tel 01 44 55 60 00, pariscityvision.com) 🎟 Château (limited areas only) moderate; courtyard, gardens and park free

Renaissance-style splendor at Fontainebleau

City Tours

This section contains self-guided tours that will help you explore the sights in each of the city's regions. Each tour is designed to take a day, with a map pinpointing the recommended places along the way. There is a quick reference guide at the end of each tour, listing everything you need in that region, so you know exactly what's close by.

CITY TOURS

81

Around the Tour Eiffel

Long vistas and grandiose public buildings characterize this part of Paris—but at its heart the Eiffel Tower is 324m (1,063ft) of pure, unmissable fun.

Morning
Start in front of the **Musée d'Orsay** (▷ 36–37), but save the museum itself for another day. The Musée National de la Légion d'Honneur across the street sets the tone for a walk that's rich in political and military landmarks. Continue along the quai Anatole France to the Assemblée Nationale, France's lower house of parliament, its dignified neoclassical portico facing the **place de la Concorde** (▷ 50–51) across the river. Continue along quai d'Orsay past the mansion-like ministry of foreign affairs, popularly known by its address and one of the most important architectural monuments of the Second Empire. Until 1973 it was also a residence for high officials; King Juan Carlos of Spain was the last to stay there. Admire the florid, gilded statuary of the **Pont Alexandre III** (▷ 73) before turning left down broad, stately avenue du Maréchal Galliéni, named for a World War I military commander. Ahead of you is the wide, imposing facade of **Les Invalides** (▷ 69)—built by Louis XIV and the last resting place of Napoleon Bonaparte.

Late morning
Take time to explore the **Musée de l'Armée** (▷ 69), which occupies much of the majestic Les Invalides, before visiting France's national military pantheon, the **Église du Dôme** (▷ 69), in which Napoleon's tomb takes pride of place.

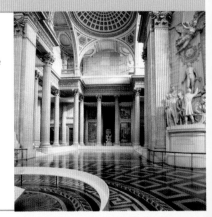

Lunch

There's a simple but strategically located café on the south side of the Musée de l'Armée, but for a more substantial lunch in elegant surroundings make a short detour to the **Brasserie Thoumieux** (▷ 146) in rue Saint-Dominique.

Afternoon

Stroll the short distance along avenue de Tourville to reach the enormous École Militaire, constructed during the time of Louis XV and still occupied by the military. It faces the **Parc du Champ de Mars** (▷ 72–73), a vast green space stretching northwest toward the Eiffel Tower. To reach the park, cross the broad cobbled avenue de la Motte-Picquet with care. Amble the length of the Champs de Mars to reach the **Eiffel Tower** (▷ 60–61); buy your tickets in advance online to save time.

Late afternoon

No visit to the Eiffel Tower is complete without crossing the river to experience the classic view of the tower itself. Cross the Pont d'Iéna to reach the **Palais de Chaillot** (▷ 72); save its museums for another day, but go up to the piazza between the two curved wings of the complex for the best view.

Evening

Stick around until after dusk to experience the beauty of the tower's soft golden lighting—and the spectacle of 20,000 flashing lights that make it glitter for five minutes every hour on the hour.

Rue St-Didier

Musée National des
Arts Asiatiques-Guimet

Musée
Galliéra

Alma-Marceau

Avenue Montaigne

Avenue Jean Go

4

Place d'Iéna

AVENUE DU PRÉSIDENT WILSON

Cours Albe

Cours Albe

Palais
de Tokyo

**Musée d'Art
Moderne de la
Ville de Paris**

AVENUE KLÉBER

AVENUE DU PRÉSIDENT WILSON

Iéna

Rue Freycinet

Rue de Longchamp

Rue Galilée

Rue de la Longchamp

**Pont de
l'Alma**

Place du
Trocadéro et du
11 Novembre 1918

AVENUE DU PRÉSIDENT WILSON

Rue de Chaillot

Rue de Magdebourg

Rue Albert de Mun

AVENUE DE NEW YORK

Pont de
l'Alma (RER)

Les Be

Passerelle
Debilly

Quai de New York

Pont des Bergès (RER)

QUAI D'OR

Trocadéro

CHAILLOT

QUAI BRANLY

Quai d'Orsay

**Palais de
Chaillot**

Rue de la Manutention

Rue Cognacq-Jay

Jardins du
Trocadéro

**Musée du
quai Branly**

Rue de l'Unive

5

Rue de l'Université

Franco-Russe

AVENUE RAPP

AV DES
NATIONS-
UNIES

PONT D'IÉNA

QUAI BRANLY

AVENUE DE LA BOURDONNAIS

R Edmond
Valentin

Passage Landrieu

Rue Ma

BLVD DELESSERT

R Chardin

Seine

AVENUE DE

QUAI BRANLY

**Tour
Eiffel**

Rue de Montessuy

Rue du
Général
Camou

Rue St-Dominique

Rue St-Dominique

Champ de Mars-
Tour Eiffel (RER)

Av Gustave Eiffel

Avenue Anatole France

Avenue Élisée Reclus

Rue Adrienne Lecouvreur

AVENUE DE LA BOURDONNAIS

Rue de Grenelle

AVENUE BOSQUET

Rue Ra

R Ro

6

**Pont de
Bir-Hakeim**

QUAI BRANLY

Avenue de Suffren

Avenue Charles Floquet

Place
Jacques
Rueff

Avenue Anatole France

Avenue Pierre Loti

Av Joseph Bouvard

Av Adrienne Lecouvreur

Allée Thomy Thierry

Rue Jean Rey

Bir-
Hakeim

Rue de la Fédération

Avenue Charles Floquet

Avenue de Suffren

**Parc du
Champ de Mars**

R Trécerie
la Pai

Allée des Cygnes

QUAI DE GRENELLE

Rue Nélaton

Rue St-Saëns

Rue du Docteur Finlay

Rue de la Fédération

BOULEVARD DE GRENELLE

Rue Desaix

Rue Edgar Faure

Rue de Presles

PLACE JOFFRE

**École
Militaire**

Avenue de Suffren

7

Rue Sextius
Michel

Rue du Docteur Finlay

Rue Viala

Jardin
Nicole de
Hautecloque

Rue Dupleix

Av de
Champaubert

Avenue de la Motte-Picquet

Avenue de Lowendal

Square
Bela-
Bartok

Rue Beatrix
Dussane

Rue Cler

Rue George
Bizet

Bouchut

R Desaix

R Clodion

R Stern
R Humblot

Place
Dupleix

R de Presles

AV DE LA MOTTE-PICQUET

Rue de Suffren

Avenue de

Rue du Théâtre

Rue Juge

Rue Fondary

Dupleix

BOULEVARD DE GRENELLE

Rue du Général
de Larminat

La Motte-
Picquet-
Grenelle

Rue du Laos

8

Charles
Michels

AVENUE ÉMILE ZOLA

Rue Violet

Rue du Théâtre

Rue Fallempin

Rue Tiphaine

Rue Letellier

Rue du Commerce

RUE FRÉMICOURT

Rue de la Croix Nivert

Cambronne

BOULEVARD GAR

Rue St-Cinoux

Rue de l'Église

Place du
Commerce

Rue des Entrepreneurs

Pass des Écoliers

Rue Cronne

Commerce

Rue Fondary

Rue Letellier

Avenue
Émile Zola

AVENUE ÉMILE ZOLA

Rue de la Croix Nivert

Nivert

Rue Cambronne

Rue Miollis

Rue Franco

Square
Violet

Rue du Commerce

Rue Lakanal

Rue
Mademoiselle

Rue Dulong
R Joseph
Liouville

Rue de l'Amiral Roussin

Rue de la Procession

Robert
Fleury

Villa Poirier

9

Boucicaut

RUE DE LA CONVENTION

Place
Étienne
Pernet

Félix Faure

Rue de Javel

Av Félix Faure

Rue de Javel

Rue des Volontaires

Square
St-Lambert

Rue Lecourbe

Rue Jean
Formigé

RUE LECOURBE

Rue Blomet

RUE DE VAUGIRARD

Place
Adolphe
Chérioux

Rue Blomet

Rue Cambronne

0 ———————— 500 m

0 ———————— 500 yds

(A)   **(B)**   **(C)**

Around the Tour Eiffel
Quick Reference Guide

Musée d'Orsay (▷ 36)
The architectural merit of this audacious conversion of a former railway station still divides opinion, but its breathtaking collection makes it one of Paris's must-see attractions.

Musée du quai Branly (▷ 40)
The national collection of art from Africa, Asia, Oceania and the Americas is housed in a modernist building by superstar architect Jean Nouvel and set in luxuriant gardens.

Musée Rodin (▷ 42)
An 18th-century mansion and its peaceful garden provide the setting for the sculptures left to the nation by Rodin, along with other works by him and contemporaries.

Tour Eiffel (▷ 60)
Though it was originally built as a temporary structure for the 1889 Exposition Universelle, it's hard to imagine Paris now without Gustave Eiffel's instantly recognizable tower.

CITY TOURS

Les Invalides

Latin Quarter, St-Germain and Islands

The area's literary and philosophical associations lend intellectual luster to this tour of the Left Bank; fashion and fine dining bring Parisian élan to the mix; and the loveliness of the Seine and its islands adds a final dash of romance.

Morning

Start at rue Mouffetard, where the wonderful food and wine shops ensure a bustling atmosphere from morning onwards. Make your way to the church of **Saint Étienne-du-Mont** (▷ 67), worth a quick peek for its flamboyant late Gothic choir, before visiting the **Panthéon** (▷ 72), whose stately neoclassical dome dominates the Latin Quarter— Paris's university district. A gentle stroll down rue Soufflot brings you to the main entrance to the **Jardin du Luxembourg** (▷ 22–23). Do as the locals do and read in the sun.

Mid-morning

Leave the park by the exit on busy rue de Vaugirard, then follow the gently curving rue Servandoni and rue Palatine to reach **Église Saint-Sulpice** (▷ 68), another Left Bank church well worth a look—this time for its cathedral-like internal dimensions. From here to the boulevard St-Germain the streets are full of intriguing boutiques; indulge in a spot of window-shopping at the stores of talented French designers **Marie Mercié** (▷ 128) or **Sonia Rykiel** (▷ 129), then polish your intellectual credentials with a leisurely drink on the terrace of **Café Les Deux Magots** (▷ 66) or **Café de Flore** (▷ 66)—these famous cafés were once the haunts of Jean-Paul Satre and Simone de Beauvoir.

Late morning

The church of **Saint-Germain-des-Prés** (▷ 67)
gives its name to one of Paris's most atmospheric
quarters, wedged between boulevard St-Germain
and the river. The streets are lined with handsome
old houses and dotted with small art galleries and
antiques shops; tucked into rue de Furstenberg is
the Musée National Eugène Delacroix.

Lunch

This is an excellent part of town in which to break for lunch. There's
plenty to tempt you, including the big brasserie buzz of **Alcazar**
(▷ 144) or the hip fusion cuisine of **Ze Kitchen Galerie**
(▷ 151)—both innovative and convivial lunchtime retreats.

Afternoon

Follow rue Dauphine to the **Pont Neuf** (▷ 74), crossing to the Île de
la Cité to soak up the sun in the beautiful **square du Vert-Galant**
(▷ 75), a tiny park on the island's western tip that offers wonderful
views along the Seine. Afterwards, skirt the Île's north bank past the
brooding bulk of the **Conciergerie** (▷ 18–19), a former royal palace,
fortress and prison. Like the church of **Sainte-Chapelle** (▷ 56–57), it
now forms part of the Palais de Justice. Slow the pace to admire the
colors of the **Marché aux Fleurs** (▷ 128) before turning down rue
de la Cité to reach the cathedral of **Notre-Dame** (▷ 44–45).

Late afternoon

Visiting the cathedral is free, but there's a charge to climb the towers,
so leave this for another day. Instead, admire the flying buttresses
from ground level and find the small copper Point Zero des Routes
de France, from where all French map distances are measured.

Evening

The soft light of evening casts a
particularly alluring spell over the **Île
Saint-Louis** (▷ 68), for many visitors
one of Paris's most romantic corners.
Stroll its embankments to enjoy views of
Notre-Dame and the Seine before cross-
ing back to the Left Bank for dinner at
La Tour d'Argent (▷ 151).

TOUR D'ARGENT

Arc de Triomphe
du Carrousel

Pyramide
du Louvre

Musée du Louvre

QUAI FRANÇOIS MITTERRAND

OUAI VOLTAIRE

QUAI DU LOUVRE

Seine

Pont
des Arts

**Seine
Boat Trip**

**Pont
Neuf**

QUAI MALAQUAIS

QUAI DE CONTI

Institut
de France

**Square du
Vert-Galant**

Rue du Bac

Pont Royal

PONT DU CARROUSEL

Rue de Beaune

Rue de Lille

Rue de Verneuil

Rue de l'Université

Rue du Pré aux Clercs

Rue des Sts-Pères

Rue Jacob

Rue Bonaparte

Rue des Beaux-Arts

Rue de Seine

Rue Visconti

Rue Mazarine

Rue Guénégaud

Monnaie
de Paris

QUAI DES GRANDS AUGUSTINS

QUAI DES ORFÈVRES

Pont Neuf-
La Monnaie

Louvre-
Rivoli

St-Germain
l'Auxerrois

RUE

RUE DE L'AMIRAL DE COLIGNY

Quai de l'Ho

Pa
de Ju

**Sain
Chap**

**ST-GERMAIN-
DES-PRÉS**

Musée National
Eugène Delacroix

R de
l'Abbaye

Rue Jacob

Alcazar

Ze
Kitchen
Galerie

Rue
Dauphine

Rue de
Savoie

Rue
Christine

**BLVD Café de Flore &
Café Les Deux Magots**

Maison
de Verre

Rue des Sts-Pères

Sonia Rykiel

ST-GERMAIN

St-Germain-
des-Prés

R Gozlin

**Saint-Germain-
des-Prés**

Rue de Buci

Jacques
Cagna

Mariage
Frères

Rue Séguier

Rue St-André des Arts

Rue de
l'Éperon

Rue Suger

Rue de
l'Ancienne
Comédie

Mabillon

R Clément

Rue Mabillon

Rue de Seine

BOULEVARD

ST-GERMAIN

Odéon

Rue Danton

Mich

Rue du Dragon

Rue du Four

RUE DE RENNES

Rue du Vieux Colombier

Rue Bonaparte

Rue
Lobineau

Rue St-Sulpice

**Rue du
Cherche-
Midi**

St-Sulpice

Place
St-Sulpice

**Saint-
Sulpice**

Marie
Mercié

Rue Palatine

Rue Garancière

Rue Servandoni

Rue Férou

Rue de Tournon

Rue de Condé

Rue de l'Odéon

Place de
l'Odéon

Rue Casimir
Delavigne

Rue Monsieur
le Prince

Rue de l'École de Médecine

BOULEVARD ST-MICHEL

**Musé
National d
Moyen Âg**

Rue Racine

Rue Champollion

Rue de la Sorbonne

Sorb

Rue Coëtlogon

Rue de Mézières

Rue Cassette

Rue Madame

Rue de Vaugirard

Place de
la Sorbonne

Rue Cujas

Rue de Vaugirard

Rue de Fleurus

Rue d'Assas

Rue de Médicis

**Palais du
Luxembourg**

Rue Soufflot

RUE ST-JACQUES

BOULEVARD ST-MICHEL

BLVD RASPAIL

Rue J-K Huysmans

Notre-Dame-
des-Champs

*Jardin du
Luxembourg*

Luxembourg
(RER)

Rue Pierre-
Collard

Rue Gay-Lussac

Rue des
St-Jacqu

Rue Pi
Marie

0   500 m
0   500 yds

Rue Auguste Comte

Vavin

Rue Vavin

Rue Bréa

Rue J Chaplain

Rue de la
Grande
Chaumière

Rue Joseph Bara

Rue Le Verrier

Rue Notre-Dame des Champs

Avenue de l'Observatoire

Avenue de l'Observatoire

Rue Michelet

Rue d'Assas

Rue Henri Barbusse

BOULEVARD

Rue de l'Abbé de l'Épée

Rue Gay-Lussac

Rue Lo
Thuill

Rue des
Ursulines

Rue des Feuillantines

RUE ST-JACQUES

Rue du Val de Grâce

BLVD RASPAIL

Rue Huyghens

BOULEVARD DU MONTPARNASSE

Port Royal
(RER)

(5) **(6)** **(7)** **(8)** **(9)**

G **H**

Latin Quarter, St-Germain and Islands
Quick Reference Guide

TOP 25 SIGHTS AND EXPERIENCES

Conciergerie (▷ 18)
Part medieval palace, part prison, this impressive but grim place preserves poignant memories of the victims of the French Revolution, including Marie-Antoinette.

Jardin du Luxembourg (▷ 22)
The epitome of French landscaping, this garden was commissioned by Marie de Médicis in 1615 and designed to remind her of her childhood Florentine home.

Musée National du Moyen-Âge (▷ 34)
A turreted 15th-century mansion provides an appropriate setting for the national collection of medieval and Gothic art.

Notre-Dame (▷ 44)
Gargoyles, flying buttresses and a 93m (305ft) spire enrich the exterior of this famous cathedral; climb the towers to see its dramatic Gothic architecture up close.

Sainte-Chapelle (▷ 56)
Hidden within the Palais de Justice is a delicate late Gothic gem: Louis IX's soaring royal chapel, with a star-studded roof and breathtaking stained glass.

Seine Boat Trip (▷ 58)
Your feet will appreciate the rest as you watch the most important sights of Paris float gently by on a romantic one-hour boat trip along the River Seine.

Marais and Bastille

Contemporary art meets high fashion in Paris's trendiest district, yet alongside the *branché* (hippest) boutiques and bars the Marais preserves magnificent architecture and is the heart of the city's Jewish life.

Morning

Start with a late breakfast on the terrace at the chic **Café Beaubourg** (▷ 66) and ponder the audacious design of the **Centre Georges Pompidou** (▷ 16–17), which caused quite a stir with its exposed ductwork and glass-roofed escalators when it opened in 1977. Today isn't the day to visit; instead, admire the jaunty Fontaine Stravinsky before walking the length of the museum, turning right into rue Rambuteau to reach the **Musée d'Art et d'Histoire du Judaïsme** (▷ 69–70) on rue du Temple. Housed in a grand 17th-century mansion or *hôtel particulier*, the museum documents European Jewish history and art from the Middle Ages onwards.

Late morning

Rue Rambuteau runs into rue des Francs-Bourgeois, graced by more aristocratic town houses. Turn left up **rue Vieille-du-Temple** (▷ 75) to discover some of the Marais' hip designer stores, including **Vanessa Bruno** (▷ 129) at No.100, now a temple to shopping. Turn right into rue Debelleyme and right again to reach the **Musée Picasso** (▷ 38–39), housed in another mansion, the elegant Hôtel Salé. Continue along rue Thorigny to rue Elzévir, where the 16th-century Hôtel Donon houses the **Musée Cognacq-Jay** (▷ 71), whose 18th-century paintings and *objets d'art* were assembled by the owner of the Samaritaine department store. Back on rue des Francs-Bourgeois, the **Hôtel Carnavalet** (▷ 28) also dates from the 16th century and comprises one half of Paris's splendid museum of local history, the **Musée Carnavalet** (▷ 28–29). Admire the architecture, but save the interior for another day.

Lunch

If the Marais's trendy shops have drained your funds, the inexpensive Jewish restaurants along **rue des Rosiers** (▷ 75) will be a welcome sight. **L'As du Fallafel** (▷ 145) at No. 34 is generally reckoned to serve the best falafel (mashed chickpeas formed into a ball and deep fried) in the city, but don't come here on Saturday—it's closed.

Afternoon

Retrace your steps to rue des Francs-Bourgeois, continuing as far as **place des Vosges** (▷ 52–53). This beautiful formal square dates from the early 17th century and is the best preserved in Paris; in the southeast corner, Victor Hugo's house is now a museum. Rue de Birague leads from the south side of the square to busy rue Saint-Antoine; to the left is the place de la Bastille, former site of the infamous prison and now dominated by the ultramodern **Opéra Bastille** (▷ 138). To the right, the Hôtel de Béthune-Sully is among the most magnificent of all the Marais's mansions; you can't visit the interior—now occupied by the Ministry of Culture—but you can admire the court and elegant garden. Continue along rue Saint-Antoine and rue François-Miron to reach the **Mémorial de la Shoah** (▷ 69), on rue Geoffroy l'Asnier—a somber counterpoint to the Musée d'Art et d'Histoire du Judaïsme.

Dinner

Bofinger (▷ 146) is one of Paris's most historic brasseries and a memorable spot for dinner. Afterwards, stay in the Marais for a drink in one of the area's lively cafés and bars—many of them popular with the city's gay and lesbian community.

Marais and Bastille
Quick Reference Guide

Centre Georges Pompidou (▷ 16)
The museum houses the national collection of modern and contemporary art, from fauvism, cubism and surrealism to Pop Art and works by the stars of the contemporary art scene. The building includes a library, cinema, bookshops and a chic restaurant.

Musée Carnavalet (▷ 28)
There is no better place to plunge into the history of Paris than the Musée Carnavalet, with period rooms and objects up to the 20th century. The section dealing with the Revolution is particularly gripping—figures such as Robespierre are brought vividly to life in their historical context.

Musée Picasso (▷ 38)
Some 500 works by Picasso are displayed in this historic Marais mansion, following a thorough refurbishment by architect Jean-François Bodin that has tripled the exhibition area and improved access for visitors with disabilities. It boasts one of the world's finest collections of work by the artist.

Place des Vosges (▷ 52)
Dating from 1612 and built on the site of a 14th-century royal palace that was abandoned and demolished by Catherine de Médicis after her husband Henri II died there, this handsome square of arcaded redbrick houses overlooks a central garden. Famous former residents include Victor Hugo.

Louvre and Champs-Élysées

Dress to impress for this route through the very heart of Paris, where iconic landmarks and glamorous designer shopping ensure there's plenty of interest along the way.

Morning
Start with a late breakfast on the terrace of the **Café Marly** (▷ 146) at the **Louvre** (▷ 30–31). You'll probably want to set aside another day to see the collection but this is a fine vantage point from which to admire the splendid setting and the audacity of I.M. Pei's modernist glass pyramid. Cross the busy place du Carrousel du Louvre to reach the Arc de Triomphe du Carrousel—not the famous triumphal arch but a smaller version, Roman in its inspiration and built in 1805 to celebrate Napoleon's victories. Beyond it, there's a dramatic view along Paris's monumental axis—west through the **Jardin des Tuileries** (▷ 24–25), across the **place de la Concorde** (▷ 50–51) and up the avenue des Champs-Élysées to the Arc de Triomphe and the distant **Grande Arche** (▷ 76) at La Défense. Paris's most central park, the Jardin des Tuileries has been a UNESCO World Heritage Site since 1991. Two galleries—the **Orangerie** (▷ 51) and **Jeu de Paume** (▷ 51)—offer an excellent excuse to linger a while.

Mid-morning
Leave the Jardin des Tuileries at the Carrousel du Louvre exit and cross rue de Rivoli, walking straight ahead along the avenue de l'Opera. Turn right into rue Richelieu and immediately on your right is the ornate facade of the **Comédie-Française** (▷ 136), famed for its classical theater. Behind the building, discover the historic gardens of the **Domaine National du Palais Royal** (▷ 66–67). Return to Avenue de l'Opera and turn right into rue Saint-Honoré to browse and window-shop. No. 233 is home to luggage-maker **Goyard** (▷ 126). At the corner of place Vendôme, look right to see one of the most elegant squares in the city. Beyond rue Royale, rue

Saint-Honoré becomes **rue du Faubourg Saint-Honoré** (▷ 74), home to the Élysée palace—official residence of the French president—and to some of Paris's most luxurious designer boutiques. Avenue Matignon continues the luxury theme but with fine art galleries and antique dealers instead of fashion, with a 44m (144ft) bronze column in its center.

Lunch

The chic 8th *arrondissement* offers plenty of good options for a leisurely and elegant lunch, while **6 New York** (▷ 144) is a suitably stylish, contemporary choice.

Afternoon

The window-shopping shifts up a gear on the far side of the Rond Point des Champs-Élysées along avenue Montaigne. Here, **Dior** (▷ 125) and **Chanel** (▷ 124) both have splendid flagship stores in which to lose half a day, and the array of designer labels is enough to constitute a serious hazard to your bank balance. Turn right off avenue Montaigne up rue François 1er to reach the broad avenue des Champs-Élysées, Paris's most famous boulevard. It ends at place de l'Étoile, dominated by the stately bulk of the **Arc de Triomphe** (▷ 14–15). Quite aside from its significance as a national monument, the Arc also makes an excellent platform for views across the city.

Rue Fortuny

AVENUE DE VILLIERS

Villiers

Parc de Monceau

Musée
Cernuschi

Musée Nissim de
Camondo

BOULEVARD DE COURCELLES

Courcelles

Monceau

Place des
Ternes

BOULEVARD

DE COURCELLES

AVENUE DES TERNES

Ternes

AVENUE DE WAGRAM

①

BOULEVARD HAUSSMANN

AVENUE HOCHE

②

Musée
Jacquemart-
André

Charles de Gaulle (+RER)

AVENUE DE FRIEDLAND

Arc de
Triomphe

CHAMPS-ÉLYSÉES

ST-HONORÉ

AV KLÉBER

Promenade des Champs-Elysées

George V

Rue du Faubourg St-Honoré

St-Philippe
du Roule

Rue du
Faubourg
Saint-Honoré

③

AVENUE D'IÉNA

AVENUE MARCEAU

Promenade des Champs-Elysées

AVENUE DES CHAMPS-ÉLYSÉES

Palais
de l'Ély

Rond-Point des
Champs-Elysées Marcel-Dassault

Franklin-D
Roosevelt

AVENUE

Champs-Elysées-
Clemenceau

Jardin
Champs

Musée
Baccarat

Chanel
Impasse
d'Antin

Dior

Place
François 1er

④

Musée
Galliéra

Palais de la
Découverte

Petit
Palais

Grand
Palais

Palais
de Tokyo

Musée d'Art
Moderne de la
Ville de Paris

6 New York

AVENUE DU PRÉSIDENT WILSON

Alma-Marceau

Cours Albert 1er

VOIE

Pont de
l'Alma

AVENUE DE NEW YORK

Cours Albert 1er

Cours La Reine
GEORGES

POMP

Pont
Alexandre III

Les Ber

Place
d'Iéna

Iéna

AVENUE D'IÉNA

Seine

Les Berges

QUAI D'ORSAY

QUAI D'ORSAY

Asse
Nat

⑤

Musée du
quai Branly

Pont de
l'Alma (+RER)

QUAI BRANLY

AVENUE DE LA BOURDONNAIS

Rue de l'Université

Rue Cognacq-Jay

Rue Robert Schumann

Rue de l'Université

Invalides (+RER)

Rue de Constantine

Tour
Eiffel

⑥

Place
Jacques
Rueff

AVENUE DE SUFFREN

AVENUE DE LA MOTTE-PICQUET

RUE DE GRENELLE

La Tour Maubourg

Varenne

Les Invalides

Mus
Rod

AVENUE

DE TOURVILLE

INVALI

⑦

Parc du
Champ de Mars

PLACE JOFFRE

École
Militaire

Duplex

B

C

D

Louvre and Champs-Élysées
Quick Reference Guide

 SIGHTS AND EXPERIENCES

Arc de Triomphe (▷ 14)
With 12 of Haussmann's avenues radiating from it, this arch is the focus of national pride and a memorial to France's war dead, with a Memorial Flame at its base.

Galerie Vivienne and the Passages Couverts (▷ 20)
A network of 19th-century shopping arcades allows you to stroll and people-watch under cover.

Jardin des Tuileries (▷ 24)
One of the most popular parks for Parisians was first laid out in the 16th century. It is a delightful place in which to relax.

Musée du Louvre (▷ 30)
The world's largest museum is a dazzling experience, from the modernist glass pyramid over its entrance to the world-famous treasures it contains.

Opéra Palais Garnier (▷ 46)
Charles Garnier's wedding cake of a building is as sumptuous as an opera house should be, with a foyer and grand staircase every bit as majestic as the auditorium itself.

Place de la Concorde (▷ 50)
A maelstrom of traffic today, this vast open space was the site of the gruesome guillotine during the French Revolution.

Montmartre

Art meets raffish nightlife, picturesque views and stepped streets in this remarkably village-like corner of the city.

CITY TOURS

Morning

Wear comfortable shoes—the route is mostly downhill and avoids steps as far as possible, but this is still the highest point in the city; the slopes can be steep and the streets are cobbled in places. Take the Métro to Abbesses station; it's the city's deepest, with a lovely original art nouveau canopy. Window-shop your way from **place des Abbesses** (▷ 73) past small, funky boutiques in rue Yvonne le Tac and rue Tardieu to reach the funicular. One of the area's celebrated stepped streets runs parallel to it, but the railway is easier on your feet. Journey's end is the distinctive, white hilltop basilica of **Sacré-Cœur** (▷ 54–55). It's one of Paris's most visited attractions and the crush inside can sometimes mar the experience. What doesn't disappoint is the breathtaking view over the city—whether from the dome or from the terrace in front of the church.

Late morning

Follow rue du Cardinal Guibert along the side of the church, braving the tourist hubbub of rue Chevalier de la Barre to reach calmer, prettier rue Cortot. Here, the **Musée de Montmartre** (▷ 71) documents the history and artistic associations of the area, which in the 19th century became a popular place of entertainment. Continue along rue Cortot to the junction with rue des Saules—if you haven't already caught a glimpse of Montmartre's vineyard, it's just downhill to the right. Turn uphill along rue des Saules then left into rue Norvins to reach busy **place du Tertre**, famous for its portrait painters.

Lunch

This is an unashamedly touristy part of Montmartre, with no shortage of places to eat, though there are many cafés with daily menus of variable quality; **Au Clair de la Lune** (▷ 145) in rue Poulbot is one of the nicest options, tucked away off place du Tertre. Arrive early in summer to make sure you get one of the tables outside.

Afternoon

From rue Poulbot, turn left down rue Norvins to reach the Radet, the first of Montmartre's windmills, at the top of rue Lepic; there were once 14 but now this and the nearby Blute Fin are the last survivors. Together they constitute the **Moulin de la Galette**, which during its time as a dance hall was painted by Renoir. It is now a restaurant. Continue downhill on rue Lepic, turning sharply right at its junction with rue des Abbesses to reach the **Cimetière de Montmartre** (▷ 66), where the roll call of famous names rivals that of Père Lachaise.

Evening

Rue des Abbesses and the surrounding streets hum with life in the evening; catch a film at **Studio 28** (▷ 139), enjoy dinner at **Seb'on** (▷ 151) or dinner and a show at **Michou** (▷ 138). Later and livelier nightlife—from rock concerts to discos and sleazy sex clubs—is found at the foot of rue des Martyrs on place Pigalle and boulevard de Clichy, the latter dominated by the famous **Moulin Rouge** (▷ 138) club.

Rue Legendre
Rue d'Oslo
Rue Coysevox
Square Carpeaux
Rue
Marcadé

Rue Davy
Rue Lamarck
Rue Carpeaux
Rue Carpeaux
Carrière
Rue Lamarck
Rue Lam

Rue Legendre
Rue Etex
Rue du Capitaine Madon
Rue de la Barrière Blanche
Rue Eugène
Rue Félix Ziem
Rue Dannémont
Rue Lam

AVENUE DE ST-OUEN
Villa St-Michel
Rue Fauvet
Rue Joseph de Maistre
R.Stanien
Rue Caulaincourt
Avenue Ju
Simon Der

AVENUE DE CLICHY
R Étienne Jodelle
Rue Ganneron
Rue Tourlaque
Avenue Ju

La Fourche
R Pierre Ginier
Rue Hégésippe Moreau
Cimetière de Montmartre
Rue Lepic
Le Moulin de la Galett

AVENUE DE CLICHY
Rue Hélène
Rue Lemercier
Rue Lécluse
Rue Lamandé
Rue Ganneron
Rue Cavallotti
Rue Caulaincourt
R Joseph de Maistre
Rue Lepic
Rue Constance
Rue Thiolaz
Sq de la B.
Rue Burc

Rue des Dames
Rue Blot
Rue Capron
P Forest
Rue Cauchois
Rue Caulaincourt
Rue Le Planquette
Rue Robert
Rue Véron
Rue des Appese
Studio 28

BOULEVARD DES BATIGNOLLES
AVENUE DE CLICHY
Dancet
BOULEVARD DE CLICHY
Moulin Rouge
Rue Puget
Coustou
Rue Germ

R de Florence
Rue de Turin
Clapeyron
RUE DE ST-PÉTERSBOURG
Place de Clichy
R Pierre Haret
R de Bruxelles
Blanche
BOULEVARD

Place de Dublin
Rue d'Amsterdam
Rue de Clichy
R de Bruxelles
Rue de Douai
Rue de Calais
RUE BLANCHE
Rue Pierre Fontaine
Rue Fromentin
Rue Duperré
P

Rue de Moscou
Rue de Turin
Rue de Vintimille
Rue Ballu
Rue de Douai
Rue Duperré

Liège
Rue de Liège
R de Parme
Rue Jules Lefebvre
Square Moncey
Rue Chaptal
Rue Paul Escudier
Rue Henner
P

Rue de Liège
Rue Moncey
Rue La Bruyère
Pigalle
Rue La Bruyère
Rue Notre

RUE DE LONDRES
Rue de Milan
0 ——— 200 m
0 ——— 200 yds
RUE BLANCHE
Rue Jean-Baptiste
Rue de la Rochefoucauld
Plac Geo

Rue d'Athènes
Rue de Clichy
P
Rue d'Aumale
Musée Gustave Moreau

GARE ST-LAZARE
Rue d'Amsterdam
RUE DE LONDRES
Rue de la Tour des Dames
Rue St-Lazare
Taitbout
RUE

St-Lazare
RUE ST-LAZARE
Place d'Estienne d'Orves
Trinité d'Estienne d'Orves
RUE DE LA CHAUSSÉE D'ANTIN
Rue de la Victoire

Haussmann-St-Lazare (RER)
(a)
(b)

Montmartre Quick Reference Guide

SIGHTS AND EXPERIENCES

Sacré-Cœur (▷ 54)

Neo-Romanesque and Byzantine in style, the white basilica of Sacré-Cœur is one of the most familiar features of the Parisian skyline, looking down on the city from its lofty hilltop perch. Built as a memorial to the dead of the Franco-Prussian war and Paris Commune, it wasn't completed until the eve of World War I and was only consecrated in 1919. Its lovely stained-glass windows were destroyed during World War II and restored afterwards.

MORE TO SEE	64

Cimetière de Montmartre
Musée de Montmartre

Place des Abbesses

The interior of Sacré-Cœur

Tomb of Alexandre Dumas in the Cimetière de Montmartre

Montmartre

Farther Afield

Louis XIV's palace at Versailles is one excursion not to miss, while more offbeat charm is to be found in the outer *arrondissements* of the city's north and east.

DAY 1
Morning
Take RER Line C to Versailles Rive Gauche and then stroll the short distance to the **Château de Versailles** (▷ 62–63). Try for an early start—the château opens at 9—and buy your ticket online to avoid a long wait in line. Start with the Grands Appartements: admire the bombastic painted ceiling of the Hall of Mirrors, which celebrates Louis XIV's military campaigns, before visiting the King's Apartment.

Lunch
If you're visiting at the weekend between April and October, exit into the gardens before midday to catch the Grandes Eaux fountains performing to music; they do the same again from 3.30 to 5.30. Afterwards, stroll down to the Grand Canal where there are formal and informal lunch options—La Flottille (tel 01 39 51 41 58, laflottille.fr) has a garden terrace by the waterside.

Afternoon
Follow the route marked on the free map to reach the **Petit Trianon** (▷ 63). Closely associated with Marie-Antoinette, this charming country estate is for many the highlight of a visit to Versailles. Explore the twee Hameau de la Reine—a play village built for the queen's amusement—before continuing through formal gardens to reach the **Grand Trianon** (▷ 63), the colonnaded marble palace where Louis XIV enjoyed trysts with his mistress, Madame de Montespan.

DAY 2
Morning
Another early start, this time for a weekend stroll through the **Marché aux Puces de Saint-Ouen** (▷ 26–27)—Paris's most famous flea market. Take Métro Line 4 to Porte de Clignancourt and cross under the Périphérique to get there by 10. Fortify yourself with coffee from one of the cafés along rue des Rosiers and pick up a free map from the tourist office at 7 impasse Simon by the Marché Paul Bert to navigate your way. Take a couple of hours to appreciate the sheer variety on offer, from secondhand clothes to elegant art deco furniture and fine art.

Lunch
Take the Métro to Barbès–Rochechouart, change to Line 2 (direction: Nation) and alight at Stalingrad. Admire the 18th-century Rotonde de la Villette and the views up the canal basin towards **Parc de la Villette** (▷ 76) before climbing hilly avenue Sécretan. Assemble a picnic from the covered market and shops here. Eat it in the **Parc des Buttes Chaumont** (▷ 76) at the top of the hill—if you're lucky, you might get one of its hillocks to yourself.

CITY TOURS

Afternoon
Descend avenue Mathurin Moreau to Colonel Fabien station. Take the Métro to Père Lachaise—there's a gate into the **Cimetière du Père-Lachaise** (▷ 48–49) directly opposite, but the main entrance is farther along boulevard de Ménilmontant. Pick up a map to find the most-visited graves, including those of Oscar Wilde, Édith Piaf and Jim Morrison, but be sure to admire the extraordinary architecture of the many tombs, too.

Early evening
Stay in the area for an apéritif or relaxed early dinner in the very vibrant rue Oberkampf. For a contemporary French bistro experience, head to dinner at **Septime** (▷ 151) close by on rue Charonne.

BOIS-COLOMBES

ASNIÈRES-
SUR-SEINE

Seine

D986

D106

D11

D109

D9

D7

LA GARENNE-
COLOMBES

D992

D106

D908

RUE MARTRE

CLICHY

D911

D110

**La Grande
Arche**

COURBEVOIE

Île de
la Jatte

LEVALLOIS-
PERRET

D9

D6

D7

D106

D7

BOULEVARD BERTHIER

B

N13

LA
DÉFENSE

D913

N13

NEUILLY-
SUR-SEINE

D908

BOULEVARD PÉRIPHÉRIQUE

N13

AVENUE CHARLES DE GAULLE

MONCEAU

Parc de
Monceau

**Fondation
Louis Vuitton**

BOULEVARD HAUSSM

D7

D1

Île de
Puteaux

ALLÉE DE LONGCHAMP

ST-HONO

AVENUE DES CHAMPS-E

Pa

CHAMPS-
ÉLYSÉES

*Lac
Inférieur*

N185

BOULEVARD LANNES

16e

CHAILLOT

QUAI BRANLY

Espla
des Inv

*Bois de
Boulogne*

**Musée
Marmottan
Monet**

INVALIDES

BOULEVARD PÉRIPHÉRIQUE

*Lac
Supérieur*

BOULEVARD SUCHET

PASSY

Parc du
Champ de Mars

AUTOROUTE DE
NORMANDIE

A13

E05

AUTEUIL

AVENUE DE VERSAILLES

QUAI ANDRÉ CITROËN

15e

BLVD EXELMANS

**Parc André-
Citroën**

GRENELLE

VAUGIRARD

ROUTE DE LA REINE

BOULEVARD VICTOR

Parc
Georges
Brassens

E05

BLVD LEFEBVRE

BOULEVARD

BOULOGNE-
BILLANCOURT

D910

Seine

Parc
Suzanne
Lenglen

D989

BOULEVARD PÉRIPHÉR

Versailles

Parc de l'Île
St-Germain

ISSY-LES-
MOULINEAUX

D50

D1

D7

Île
St-Germain

D989

VANVES

Parc
Frédéric
Pic

D906

MALAKOFF

MEUDON

D2

D72

AVENUE DE PARIS

MONTR

Cimetiè
Parisie
de Bagne

0   1 km

0   1 mile

SIGHTS AND EXPERIENCES

Marché aux Puces de Saint-Ouen (▷ 26)

The sprawling, 7ha (15-acre) Marché aux Puces de Saint-Ouen is not one market but a series of market buildings, arcades, stalls and individual dealers. Together they create an enjoyable way to spend a weekend morning alongside the locals.

Musée Marmottan Monet (▷ 32)

This 19th-century mansion is an elegant setting for a truly mesmerizing collection of Impressionist paintings, including Monet's memorable and world-renowned canvases of dappled irises, wisteria and water lilies from his last years at Giverny.

Père Lachaise (▷ 48)

The chance to see the tombs of literary, musical and artistic greats—including Frederick Chopin, Marcel Proust and, of course, Oscar Wilde—is what draws many visitors to this hilly, historic cemetery, but the wonderful architecture of its myriad tombs and vaults repays languid exploration.

Versailles (▷ 62)

The grandeur of the Sun King, Louis XIV, survives in swaggering stone form at the Château de Versailles, but the complex also offers more intimate glimpses of royal life at the estates of Grand and Petit Trianon. Despite the crowds, its rural idyll makes for a perfect day away from the city rush.

Modern design on a huge scale, La Grand Arche

Shop

Whether you're looking for the best local products, a department store or a quirky boutique, you'll find them all in Paris. In this section shops are listed alphabetically.

SHOP

Introduction

One of the world's shopping capitals, Paris is not all about luxury designer stores. Don't forget the individual shops, inexpensive chain stores, big and small flea markets and everything in between.

The Capital of Fashion

Narrow rue du Faubourg Saint-Honoré and broad, stately avenue Montaigne are the most prestigious fashion addresses in the city—the places to go for couture, luxury and high price tags, or simply for a spot of *lèche-vitrines* (window-shopping) past the beautiful displays. In these streets you'll find the top names— Gucci, Roberto Cavalli and Prada. Rue de la Paix glitters with names, including Cartier and Van Cleef et Arpels. To the north are the great Belle Époque department stores of boulevard Haussmann, Galeries Lafayette and Printemps, complete with English-speaking guides on hand.

Nip across the Seine to Saint-Germain-des-Prés for fashion with flair alongside fine art and antiques and, further south, the city's oldest department store, Le Bon Marché (▷ 123), at 24 rue de Sèvres.

The Capital of Chic

Be sure not to miss the historic *arrondissements* between the Louvre and Bastille. Fashion has colonized the area around place des Victoires in the 1st *arrondissement* with

---

GOURMET PICNICS

There isn't a word for delicatessen in French. A *charcuterie* is a pork butcher and a *traiteur* a caterer, or a shop selling ready-cooked dishes. The two are closely related and are often combined. Inside, glass cabinets or counters display dozens of exquisite freshly prepared salads, grated carrot, paper-thin slices of cucumber, aubergines (eggplant), mushrooms, meat pies and spicy sausages, as well as garlic, bean-and-pork stew and a gourmet mix of cooked meats.

Clockwise from top: Tasty choices at Le Bon Marché Rive Gauche; macaroons from Ladurée pâtisserie; sweet treats from Stohrer chocolate and pastry shop;

Marc Jacobs and Stella McCartney opening boutiques in the Palais Royal; further east, rue Étienne-Marcel is good for youth-oriented labels, while rue Vieille-du-Temple in the Marais is a must-see for its chic mix of small boutiques and intriguing concept stores.

Out of the Rain
In the Sentier and Opéra districts, explore delightful, shop-lined 19th-century arcades, full of quirky and interesting small boutiques that make them an excellent place to linger if the weather is poor.

Buy the Best
Seek out great French flair and quality, not just in fashion but also in high-quality cookware—Le Creuset saucepans, Sabatier knives, kitchen gadgets that actually work, such as a Peugeot peppermill, a fine piece of kitchen engineering—and in stylish children's and baby clothes. For epicurean delights try exquisite prepared foods from Fauchon (▷ 125) or La Grande Épicerie at Le Bon Marché, handmade chocolates and fine wines, which all make tempting buys.

Down to Earth
If luxury and high fashion are not for you there are bargains to be had, so join the locals at the legendary flea markets, starting with Marché aux Puces de Saint-Ouen (▷ 26–27).

SHOP

WHAT'S WHAT
Boulangeries sell baguettes, and more besides; try the *ficelle*, a thinner, finer loaf, or *pain au levain*, delicious sourdough bread. And then there are the croissants, *ordinaire* or *au beurre* (with butter). *Pâtisseries* sell pastries and tarts. *Charcuteries* sell cold meats, snails, cheese, truffles, wines, caviar and more. *Parfumeries* can stock solely French perfume but some sell cosmetics and soaps, too. *Bouquinistes* sell used books and prints, posters and postcards.

---

the latest shoe trends to tempt shoppers; Bleu d'Auvergne cheese for sale in the city; the enticing facade to some of the city's shops

Directory

Around the Tour Eiffel
Antiques
Galerie Captier
Department Stores
Le Bon Marché Rive Gauche

Latin Quarter, St-Germain and Islands
Books and CDs
Shakespeare and Company
Candles and Scents
Dyptyque
Clothes and Hats
Marie Mercié
Sonia Rykiel
Zadig & Voltaire
Food and Drink
Patrick Roger
Pierre Hermé
Rue Mouffetard
Markets
Marché aux Fleurs

Marais and Bastille
Art
Artazart
Clothes and Hats
Agnès B
Azzedine Alaïa
Coton Doux
Free'P'Star
Vanessa Bruno
Department Stores
BHV
Food and Drink
Mariage Frères
Home and Garden
Dehillerin
Malls
Forum des Halles

Louvre and Champs-Élysées
Accessories/Shoes
Cartier
Christian Louboutin
Goyard
Louis Vuitton
Antiques
La Galerie Fayet
Louvre des Antiquaires
Beauty
Detaille
Books and CDs
Galerie de l'Opéra de Paris
Clothes and Hats
Chanel
Colette
Didier Ludot
Dior
Department Stores
Galeries Lafayette (▷ panel, 126)
Printemps (▷ panel, 126)
Food and Drink
À la Mère de Famille
Fauchon
Stohrer
Sports/Memorabilia
Paris Saint-Germain Store
Toys
Si Tu Veux

Montmartre
Books and CDs
Librairie des Abbesses
Clothes and Hats
Petit Bateau
Food and Drink
Boulangerie Delmontel
Markets
Marché Barbès
Marché de la rue Lepic

SHOP

Shopping A-Z

À LA MÈRE DE FAMILLE

lameredefamille.com

This original 18th-century grocery shop has shelves laden with imaginatively created chocolates, jams and unusual groceries. Beautifully packaged, these edible treats make great presents to take back home. There are ten stores around the city.

🏠 H2 ✉ 33–35 rue du Faubourg Montmartre, 75009 ☎ 01 47 70 83 69 🕐 Mon–Sat 9.30–8, Sun 10–1 🚇 Le Peletier, Cadet

AGNÈS B

europe.agnesb.com

Agnès B's fashion is the epitome of young Parisian chic: sharply cut clothes with original details. French-born Agnès worked her way up from assistant fashion editor to own-name label, and her clothes are still made in France.

🏠 J4 ✉ 6 rue du Jour, 75001 ☎ 01 45 08 56 56 🕐 May–Sep Mon–Sat 10.30–7.30; Oct–Apr Mon–Sat 10–7.30 🚇 Les Halles

ARTAZART

artazart.com

Located on the banks of the Canal Saint-Martin, this bookshop specializes in design, architecture, photography and fashion. A small gallery shows work by up-and-coming artists.

🏠 M7 ✉ 83 quai de Valmy, 75010 ☎ 01 40 40 24 03 🕐 Mon–Fri 10.30–7.30, Sat 11–7.30, Sun 1–7.30 🚇 Jacques Bonsergent, République

AZZEDINE ALAÏA

alaia.fr

Alaïa, an artistic genius of the fashion world, is a Tunisian-born fashion designer with an eye for "feminine Hollywood" glamor, and

WINDOW-SHOPPING

Some Parisian streets do not fit any convenient label and so make for intriguing window-shopping. Try rue Jean-Jacques Rousseau and Passage Véro-Dodat, rue Saint-Roch, rue Monsieur-le-Prince and parallel rue de l'Odéon, rue Saint-Sulpice, rue des Francs-Bourgeois and rue du Pont-Louis-Philippe or rue de la Roquette. For luxury goods, take a stroll along the rue du Faubourg-Saint-Honoré.

the showroom is the place to come for his signature silhouette-hugging dresses.

🏠 K6 ✉ 7 rue de Moussy, 75004 ☎ 01 42 72 19 19 🕐 Mon–Sat 10–7 🚇 Hôtel de Ville

BHV

bhv.fr

You can't buy shoes in this department store, but otherwise it's famous for having everything you'll ever need, from baby clothes to an electrical transformer. You can even get your watch battery replaced should you need to.

🏠 K6 ✉ 52 rue de Rivoli, 75004 ☎ 09 77 40 14 00 🕐 Thu–Tue 9.30–8, Wed 9.30–9 🚇 Hôtel de Ville

LE BON MARCHÉ RIVE GAUCHE

lebonmarche.com

You'll find the classiest goods in this Left Bank store. The modernist interior adds to the elegant atmosphere. Don't miss the beauty shop on the ground floor or the food hall, La Grande Épicerie, in an adjoining building, which stocks delicacies from all over the world.

🏠 F7 ✉ 24 rue de Sèvres, 75007 ☎ 01 44 39 80 00 🕐 Mon–Wed, Sat 10–8, Thu–Fri 10–9 🚇 Sèvres–Babylone

SHOP

Most of the big-name designers are on rue du Faubourg Saint-Honoré and avenue Montaigne, but you'll also find women's high fashion on the place des Victoires (home to Kenzo and Victoire), the rue Étienne-Marcel and towards Les Halles. In the Marais, the best shopping runs between rue de Sévigné, rue des Rosiers, place des Vosges and side streets. In Saint-Germain, look along and off boulevard Saint-Germain, on rue de Grenelle and up boulevard Raspail.

BOULANGERIE DELMONTEL

arnaud-delmontel.com

This bakery and pastry shop stands out on a street known for its many mouthwatering food shops. Baker Arnaud Delmontel won the city's prize for best baguette in 2007 and became official supplier to the presidential residence.

🚇 C3 ✉ 39 rue des Martyrs, 75009 ☎ 01 48 78 29 33 🕐 Wed–Mon 7am–8.30pm, Sun 7–2.30 🚊 Notre-Dame-de-Lorette

CARTIER

cartier.fr

This is the traditional Paris home of the exclusive jeweler, known the world over, selling contemporary and vintage jewelry, watches, leather goods and perfumes. There's another branch right around the corner on place Vendôme.

🚇 G3 ✉ 13 rue de la Paix, 75002 ☎ 01 58 18 23 00 🕐 Mon–Sat 11–7 🚊 Opéra

CHANEL

chanel.com

Classy yet sexy, Chanel's fashion embodies Parisian style. At this main store there is everything from fashion to jewelry, leather goods, watches, sunglasses, perfume and beauty products.

🚇 D4 ✉ 42 avenue Montaigne, 75008 ☎ 01 40 70 82 00 🕐 Mon–Sat 10–7 🚊 Franklin D Roosevelt

CHRISTIAN LOUBOUTIN

christianlouboutin.com

A shoe fetishist's dream, Christian Louboutin is the place to go for exquisite women's shoes with glamor and extreme heels.

🚇 H5 ✉ 19 rue Jean-Jacques Rousseau 75001 ☎ 0800 94 58 04 🕐 Mon–Sat 10.30–7 🚊 Louvre–Rivoli

COLETTE

colette.fr

If it's at the forefront of style, you'll find it at this department store, the place to go for leading design in fashion and home furnishings. There's also a water bar with over 100 different brands to try.

🚇 G4 ✉ 213 rue Saint-Honoré, 75001 ☎ 01 55 35 33 90 🕐 Mon–Sat 11–7 🚊 Tuileries, Pyramides

COTON DOUX

cotondoux.com

You'll find pure cotton men's shirts in a kaleidoscope of colors and patterns, plus boxer shorts, silk ties, scarves and pyjamas. Coton Doux sets mainstream street style for 30-somethings and above in Paris.

🚇 K6 ✉ 24 rue de la Verrerie, 75002 ☎ 01 44 54 09 29 🕐 Mon–Sat 10–8, Sun 11–8 🚊 Hôtel de Ville

DEHILLERIN

e-dehillerin.fr

For every budding chef who visits Paris, this should be a place of pilgrimage. Come here for all your top-end kitchen needs—copper pans, knives, bains-marie, sieves and more. A mail-order service is also available.

🔲 H4 ✉ 18–20 rue Coquillière, 75001 ☎ 01 42 36 53 13 ⏰ Mon 9–12.30, 2–6, Tue–Sat 9–6 Ⓜ Les Halles, Louvre–Rivoli

DETAILLE
detaille.com

This Paris beauty shop, which celebrated its centenary in 2005, was opened by the Countess de Presle, one of the first people in Paris to own a car and the inventor of the store's best-selling antipollution face cream, Baume Automobile.

🔲 G2 ✉ 10 rue Saint-Lazare, 75009 ☎ 01 48 78 68 50 ⏰ Tue–Sat 11–2, 3–7 Ⓜ Notre-Dame-de-Lorette

DIDIER LUDOT
didierludot.fr

Good quality pre-owned vintage designer clothes (by the likes of Chanel, Dior, Balmain, Givenchy and Lanvin) and classic Hermès handbags are sold at this shop in a picturesque location.

🔲 H4 ✉ 20–24 Galerie Montpensier, 75001 ☎ 01 42 96 06 56 ⏰ Mon–Sat 10.30–7 Ⓜ Palais-Royal–Musée du Louvre

DIOR
dior.com

Dior's historic headquarters sells everything from the ready-to-wear collection to menswear, jewelry and accessories. The flagship store offers the current season range which includes classic evening wear for that extra special occasion.

🔲 C4 ✉ 30 avenue Montaigne, 75008 ☎ 01 40 73 73 73 ⏰ Mon–Sat 10–7 Ⓜ Franklin D Roosevelt

DIPTYQUE
diptyqueparis.fr

Diptyque sells the ultimate in beautifully crafted candles, in a choice of 48 exquisite scents. There's also a divine range of eaux de cologne.

🔲 J7 ✉ 34 boulevard Saint-Germain, 75005 ☎ 01 43 26 77 44 ⏰ Mon–Sat 10–7 Ⓜ Maubert–Mutualité

FAUCHON
fauchon.com

Paris's most renowned *épicerie* is a visual and gastronomic feast for foodies, complete with an excellent pâtisserie, a deli and a wine shop in imposing premises close to the Madeleine.

🔲 F3 ✉ 24–26 place de la Madeleine, 75008 ☎ 01 70 39 38 00 ⏰ Mon–Sat 10–8.30, boulangerie Mon–Sat 8am–8.30pm Ⓜ Madeleine

FORUM DES HALLES
forumdeshalles.com

This partly underground shopping complex is the biggest in central Paris and contains a few surprises —including a Muji store—among its predominantly mainstream

Vintage fashion at Didier Ludot

fashion offerings. The complex is currently undergoing extensive renovations, but remains open for business as usual.

➕ J5 ✉ 1–7 rue Pierre-Lescot, 75001
☎ 01 44 76 96 56 🕓 Mon–Sat 10–8
🚇 Châtelet-Les Halles

FREE'P'STAR
freepstar.com

There's a wonderful rummage-sale ambience at this trendy second-hand clothes shop in the Marais, where the styles range from leopardskin to military surplus. You're sure to find something unusual to wear here.

➕ K6 ✉ 61 rue de la Verrerie, 75004
☎ 01 42 78 00 76 🕓 Mon–Sat 11–9, Sun 2–9 🚇 Hôtel de Ville

GALERIE CAPTIER
galeriecaptier.com

The antique Chinese and Japanese furniture (17th to 19th century) and old Japanese screens here have been chosen by owners Bernard and Sylvie Captier, who

---

DEPARTMENT STORES

Printemps and Galeries Lafayette, in the prestigious boulevard Haussmann, each stock hundreds of brands—from fashion to designer homeware. Printemps (🕓 Mon–Wed, Fri–Sat 9.35–8, Thu 9.35–8.45 🚇 Havre-Caumartin) claims to have Europe's largest beauty department. Don't miss the art nouveau stained-glass cupola on the sixth floor of Printemps de la Mode, or the view from the ninth floor of Printemps de la Maison. At Galeries Lafayette (🕓 Mon–Sat 9.30–8, Thu until 9 🚇 Chaussée d'Antin) highlights include the 1912 Byzantine-style glass dome and the Lafayette Gourmet food hall.

---

regularly travel to Asia to search out exotic and refined works of art.

➕ G6 ✉ 33 rue de Beaune, 75007
☎ 01 42 61 00 57 🕓 Mon 2.30–7, Tue–Sat 10.30–7 🚇 Rue du Bac

LA GALERIE FAYET
galerie-fayet.com

Owned for many years by the now retired Mr Segas, this quirky but atmospheric shop selling antique walking canes is tucked into one of Paris's historic 19th-century shopping arcades. The collection has been expanded by the new owners to include high quality umbrellas.

➕ H3 ✉ 34 passage Jouffroy, 75001
☎ 01 47 70 89 65 🕓 Tue–Sat 10–12.30, 1.30–7 🚇 Grands Boulevards

GALERIE DE L'OPÉRA DE PARIS

This boutique-bookshop focuses on opera and choreography, with all the latest CDs and books, as well as postcards, posters and gifts. It's also the place to buy a set of opera glasses for the evening performance.

➕ G3 ✉ Opéra Palais Garnier, rue Halévy, 75009 ☎ 01 53 43 03 97 🕓 Daily 10–7.30 🚇 Opéra

GOYARD
goyard.com

Founded in 1792 and in the same premises since 1834, Goyard manufactures and sells some of the world's finest luggage. Beautifully crafted, rugged and a classic statement of style, these trunks and bags are underground style icons.

➕ F4 ✉ 233 rue Saint-Honoré, 75001
☎ 01 42 60 57 04 🕓 Mon–Sat 10–7
🚇 Concorde, Tuileries

LIBRAIRIE DES ABBESSES

In a city famed for its writers and novelists, independent bookshops are now a rarity, but this is a great little bookshop for those who read French or want to practice. It also sells beautiful art books.

🕂 c2 ✉ 30 rue Yvonne le Tac, 75018 ☎ 01 46 06 84 30 🕐 Mon 11–8, Tue–Fri 9.30–8, Sat 10–8, Sun 12–8 🚇 Abbesses

LOUIS VUITTON

louisvuitton.com

The ultimate brand name on the Champs-Élysées and an essential store for all fashionistas was conceived as a continuation of a promenade on the avenue.

🕂 C3 ✉ 101 avenue des Champs-Élysées, 75008 ☎ 01 53 57 52 00 🕐 Mon–Sat 10–8, Sun 11–7 🚇 George V

LOUVRE DES ANTIQUAIRES

louvre-antiquaires.com

At this huge, modernized complex of antiques shops you'll find everything from Eastern carpets to furniture, silver, porcelain and paintings. The quality is good but expect high prices.

🕂 H5 ✉ 2 place du Palais-Royal, 75001 ☎ 01 42 97 27 27 🕐 Tue–Sun 11–7 🚇 Palais-Royal–Musée du Louvre

MARCHÉ BARBÈS

Come to this colorful market for ethnic wares, scarves, fruit, vegetables and spices. Shop where the locals shop for a taste of Parisian neighborhood banter.

🕂 Off map at d2 ✉ Boulevard de la Chapelle, 75018 🕐 Wed 8–1, Sat 7–3 🚇 Barbès–Rochechouart

MARCHÉ AUX FLEURS

Housed in picturesque pavilions this flower and plant market has

Louis Vuitton on the Champs-Élysées

everything you can imagine. Thousands of pots are displayed, plus trees and shrubs.

🕂 J6 ✉ Place Louis Lépine, 75004, Île de la Cité 🕐 Mon–Sat 8–7.30 (bird market on Sun) 🚇 Cité

MARCHÉ DE LA RUE LEPIC

It's up a steep hill but worth the effort to explore this atmospheric street, made famous in the film *Amélie* (2001). The best food shops are from the junction with rue des Abbesses down to boulevard de Clichy.

🕂 b2 ✉ Rue Lepic and rue des Abbesses, 75018 🕐 Most shops open Tue–Sat 9–1, 4–7, Sun 9–1 🚇 Abbesses, Blanche

MARIAGE FRÈRES

mariagefreres.com

This teahouse, founded in 1854, offers hundreds of teas from all over the world, including some exclusive house blends. The company also sells accessories like fine porcelain tea pots and cups.

🕂 K6 ✉ 30 rue du Bourg-Tibourg, 75004 ☎ 01 42 72 28 11 🕐 Daily 10.30–7.30; tea room 12–7 🚇 Hôtel de Ville

Flower market on the Île de la Cité

MARIE MERCIÉ
mariemercie.com
Marie Mercié's handmade hats have graced the catwalks since the 1980s, for they complement the haute couture collections of the best French designers. See extravagant hats for women here, from classic to theatrical. The men's store, Anthony Peto, is at 56 rue Tiquetonne, 75002.

✚ H7 ✉ 23 rue Saint-Sulpice, 75006 ☎ 01 43 26 45 83 🕐 Mon–Sat 11–7 Ⓜ Odéon

PARIS SAINT-GERMAIN STORE
boutiquepsg.fr
Paris may be the city of romance, but it is its world-famous soccer team, Paris Saint-Germain (or PSG as it is more popularly known), that ignites the passions of Parisians. This flagship store sells a wide range of official merchandise, including replica shirts, plus a selection of PSG related memorabilia.

✚ D3 ✉ 27 ave de Champs-Élysées, 75008 ☎ 0969 32 21 62 🕐 Mon–Sat 10–10, Sun 10–9 Ⓜ Franklin D Roosevelt

PATRICK ROGER
patrickroger.com
Winner of the prestigious Meilleur Ouvrier de France (Best Craftsman in France) for chocolate products, Patrick Roger is a maverick, a sculptor of chocolate as well as a chocolate maker.

✚ H7 ✉ 108 boulevard Saint-Germain, 75006 ☎ 0963 64 50 21 🕐 Daily 10.30–7.30 Ⓜ Odéon

PETIT BATEAU
petit-bateau.com
Known for their excellent quality and fit, every grown-up Parisienne has a chic Petit Bateau T-shirt. The company is also renowned for its well-made everyday baby and children's collections.

✚ b2 ✉ 50 rue des Abbesses, 75018 ☎ 01 42 52 81 76 🕐 Mon–Sat 10–7 Ⓜ Abbesses

PIERRE HERMÉ
pierreherme.com
The couture pastries are as visually stunning as they are mouthwatering and the gold-leaf ornamented chocolate cake is legendary. Or take home a delightfully presented box of *macarons* (macaroons) as a gift.

✚ G7 ✉ 72 rue Bonaparte, 75006 ☎ 01 43 54 47 77 🕐 Daily 10–8 Ⓜ Saint-Sulpice, Mabillon

RUE MOUFFETARD
Visit this tourist classic straggling down a narrow, hilly street, for a wonderful array of shops and stalls selling fruit and veg, *charcuterie* and aromatic cheeses. Good café stops en route.

✚ J9 ✉ Rue Mouffetard, 75005 🕐 Daily, but some shops and stalls closed Sun–Mon Ⓜ Monge

SHAKESPEARE AND COMPANY

shakespeareandcompany.com

Opened in 1951, this English language bookstore quickly became a magnet for ex-pat writers and wannabe literary characters. Allen Ginsberg and Henry Miller where just two of the literary giants who spent some time here.

🚹 J7 ✉ 37 rue de la Bûcherie, 75005
☎ 01 43 25 40 93 🕐 Daily 10am–11pm
Ⓜ Saint-Michel

SI TU VEUX

situveuxjouer.com

The perfect toy shop, Si Tu Veux sells affordable toys, games and dressing-up clothes and accessories. There's a good range of options for creative play for all ages, excellent old-style wooden toys and a separate section devoted to teddy bears.

🚹 H4 ✉ 68 Galerie Vivienne, 75002
☎ 01 42 60 59 97 🕐 Mon–Sat 10.30–7
Ⓜ Bourse

SONIA RYKIEL

soniarykiel.com

In business since 1968, this classic ready-to-wear fashion house was founded by Paris-born Sonia and is now run by her daughter Nathalie. It also sells ranges of accessories and perfumes and has launched youth and children's lines.

🚹 G6 ✉ 175 boulevard Saint-Germain,
75006 ☎ 01 49 54 60 60 🕐 Mon–Sat
10.30–7 Ⓜ Saint-Germain-des-Prés

STOHRER

stohrer.fr

When the Polish wife of King Louis XV moved into Versailles palace she brought her patissier, Nicolas Stohrer, with her. Five years later he opened this shop and here, it is said, the delectable rum baba was invented.

🚹 J4 ✉ 51 rue Montorgueil, 75002
☎ 01 40 33 38 20 🕐 Daily 7.30–8.30
Ⓜ Les Halles

VANESSA BRUNO

vanessabruno.com

This designer's practical, easy-to-wear women's clothing has won her a loyal following. The 1960s and '70s inspired designs are renowned for their stylish flair. The recently launched "cabas" leather bag, has become a classic must-have item.

🚹 L5 ✉ 100 rue Vieille-du-Temple, 75003
☎ 01 42 77 19 41 🕐 Mon 12.30–7.30,
Tue–Sat 10.30–7.30, Sun 2–7 Ⓜ Filles du Calvaire

ZADIG & VOLTAIRE

zadig-et-voltaire.com

There's a trendy, youthful edge to the men's and womenswear at this Left Bank outpost of the internationally successful fashion house founded by Frenchman Thierry Gillier, son of the founder of the Lacoste empire.

🚹 G6 ✉ 200 boulevard Saint-Germain,
75005 ☎ 01 45 49 10 34 🕐 Mon–Sat
10.30–7.30 Ⓜ Saint-Germain-des-Prés

SHOP

BOUTIQUING

The streets around the Abbesses Métro station offer a treasure trove of quirky independent clothing, accessories and gift boutiques. For fabulous food shops head down the rue des Abbesses and turn left on rue Lepic. Another wonderful food shopping area in Montmartre is the stretch of rue des Martyrs that descends below the boulevard de Clichy.

Entertainment

Once you've done with sightseeing for the day, you'll find lots of other great things to do with your time in this chapter, even if all you want to do is relax with a drink. In this section establishments are listed alphabetically.

ENTERTAINMENT

Introduction

The heart of Paris has a special beauty at night, and an electric atmosphere. Boulevards, great monuments and historic buildings are dazzlingly illuminated. The Champs-Élysées, place de la Concorde and the Louvre make a magnificent spectacle of lights against the night sky. The soaring Eiffel Tower, shining like gold and glittering for five minutes every hour, and the silvery white of the Sacré-Cœur Basilica are majestic landmarks.

Nightlife by Area

In a city as big as Paris there is no single focus for nightlife, and where you go will depends a lot on what you are looking for. Small theaters and jazz clubs still dot the Left Bank, and there are more jazz clubs around Châtelet and Les Halles. While there's a chic and expensive feel to many of the bars and clubs in the west, between Étoile and Opéra, Montmartre, Pigalle and Clichy offer nightlife of an altogether more raffish kind. However their sex shops and strip joints are interspersed with mainstream discos and some of the city's best live music venues, so that despite the overt sleaze it's not an area to be written off. The eastern *arrondissements* have some of the most interesting and fashionable nightlife, from the Marais's gay scene

AN EVENING STROLL

Start at Châtelet and walk toward the Louvre along the embankment opposite the illuminated Conciergerie, the Monnaie and the Institut de France. At the Louvre make a detour into the magnificently lit Cour Carrée. Return to the river, cross the Pont des Arts, then walk back along the opposite bank, with views north of the stately Samaritaine and the Palais de Justice on the Île de la Cité. Continue toward Saint-Michel, then cross over to Notre-Dame and make your way around the north side of the island for good views.

Clockwise from top: Evening view of the domed Institut de France, with the Pont des Arts in the foreground; the Opera Bastille; cafés, bars and clubs line the streets of

and *branché* (trendy) café society to the scuffed boho chic of lively rue Oberkampf.

Glamorous Fun

There's a sense of excitement, anticipation and enjoyment in Paris. In addition to glamorous cabarets, there are world-class ballet, concert and opera venues, nightclubs, discos, café-theaters and atmospheric bars with live music. Although the Métro is closed from 1.15am (2.15 Friday and Saturday) to 5.30am, plenty of taxis run at night, as well as the Noctilien buses (ratp.fr).

Clubbing Paris Style

Dressing up—not down—is still often the rule when you go dancing in Paris, and if your clothes don't pass muster you may not get past the door at some clubs. Drinks prices can be steep but the price of entry often includes a *conso* (free drink).

Added Magic

A boat trip along the Seine between the illuminated buildings adds extra magic, and *bateaux mouches* run every evening until 10.30 (9.20 in winter). For experienced in-line skaters a high-speed three-hour skating tour of Paris takes place every Friday at 9.30pm (see pari-roller.com for details).

GAY PARIS

As befits a city which had an openly gay mayor—Bertrand Delanoë—from 2001 to 2014, Paris is a welcoming place for lesbian and gay visitors, particularly in the fashionable Marais district, where the list of gay-friendly or mixed venues stretches beyond the established confines of the official gay scene. The hugely popular Open Café (✉ 17 rue des Archives ☎ 01 48 87 80 25, opencafe.fr) and slick Raidd (✉ 23 rue du Temple ☎ 01 42 77 04 88, raiddbar.com) are two of the area's best places to see and be seen in.

Montmartre; enjoying a night out; a delightful evening scene in Paris; there are plenty of clubs to choose from; the famous Moulin Rouge

Directory

Around the Tour Eiffel

Clubs
Petit Journal Montparnasse

Latin Quarter, St-Germain and Islands

Bars
Caveau de la Huchette
Cinemas
Le Champo
Lucernaire/Centre National
  d'Art et d'Essai
Studio Galande
Classical Music
Musée National du Moyen-Âge
Clubs
Concrete
Theaters
Théâtre de la Huchette

Marais and Bastille

Cinemas
Forum des Images
Clubs
Duc des Lombards
Favela Chic
Sunset-Sunside
Opera
Opéra Bastille
Theater/Dance
Théâtre du Châtelet
Théâtre de la Ville

Louvre and Champs-Élysées

Bars
Le Bar du Bristol
Barramundi
Harry's New York Bar
Cinemas
Le Balzac
Classical Music
Auditorium du Louvre
Clubs
Le Baron
Club l'Arc
Queen
Shows
Le Crazy Horse
Theaters
Comédie Française/Salle Richelieu

Montmartre

Cinemas
Studio 28
Clubs
Michou
Contemporary Music
La Boule Noire/La Cigale
Divan du Monde
Shows
Moulin Rouge
Theaters
Bouffes du Nord

Farther Afield

Classical Music
Philharmonie de Paris

Entertainment A-Z

AUDITORIUM DU LOUVRE

louvre.fr

A high-quality series of lunchtime and evening concerts are held in this 450-seat auditorium beneath the Louvre's pyramid. Currently Wednesday evenings offers chamber music, while Thursday afternoons are dedicated to rising talent, and Friday evenings to classics and music specially commissioned by the museum.

🟦 G5 ✉ Musée du Louvre (entrance by the pyramid), 75001 ☎ 01 40 20 55 55 🔊 Palais-Royal

LE BALZAC

cinemabalzac.com

Le Balzac is famous for its screenings of American independent films (in the original language) and for the debates that often follow. Concerts are held before Saturday evening screenings. Bar on site.

🟦 B3 ✉ 1 rue Balzac, 75008 ☎ 01 45 61 10 60 🔊 George V, Charles de Gaulle–Étoile

LE BAR DU BRISTOL

lebristolparis.com

Set in the high-class Le Bristol hotel, this equally classy bar is one of the top cocktail venues in the city, whose inventive mixologist has created a menu of classic and new drinks. There are DJ sessions Tuesday to Saturday.

🟦 E3 ✉ 112 rue du Faubourg Saint-Honoré, 75008 ☎ 01 53 43 42 41 🕔 Daily 5.30pm–2am 🔊 Miromesnil

LE BARON

clublebaron.com

Once a high-class hostess club and now a popular nightspot that attracts stars and VIPs, Le Baron was founded by trendy graffiti artist André and features top DJs.

CINEPHILE'S PARADISE

With some 110 cinemas in Paris, the choice for movie-goers can be tantalizing. Foreign films shown in their original languages have VO *(version originale)* after the title. New movies come out on Wednesday, but you'll also find a selection of older and classic films in art houses. The Gaumont, MK2 and UGC cinemas offer multiple-entry cards that can be used for up to three people or more.

🟦 B4 ✉ 6 avenue Marceau, 75008 ☎ 01 47 20 04 01 🕔 Daily 11pm–dawn 🔊 Alma–Marceau, Étoile

BARRAMUNDI

barramundi.fr

Barramundi draws a fashionable crowd with its world music, bar, lounge and eclectic restaurant. This is one of Paris's top chill-out spots.

🟦 H3 ✉ 3 rue Taitbout, 75009 ☎ 01 47 70 21 21 🕔 Mon–Fri 12–3.30pm, 6.30pm–2am, Sat 7pm–5am 🔊 Richelieu–Drouot, Chaussée d'Antin

BOUFFES DU NORD

bouffesdunord.com

Once the "lost" theater of Paris, this auditorium was rescued in the 1970s by English director Peter Brook and Micheline Rozan. It's a no-frills "theater for the people" with low ticket costs, even cheaper matinee performances, and theater workshops for the local community.

🟦 Off map at d2 ✉ 37 bis boulevard de la Chapelle, 75010 ☎ 01 46 07 34 50 🔊 La Chapelle

LA BOULE NOIRE/LA CIGALE

lacigale.fr

Famous names have played at the diminutive La Boule Noire,

Numerous classical music concerts are held in churches—try Saint-Eustache, Saint-Germain-des-Prés, Saint-Julien-le-Pauvre, Saint-Louis-en-l'Île, Saint-Roch and Saint-Séverin (ampconcerts.com). Seats are reasonably priced and the quality of music is sometimes very high. May to September free concerts are held in parks. Schedules are available at the Office du Tourisme or the Hôtel de Ville.

including Franz Ferdinand, Jamie Cullum and Metallica. It's linked to a former theater, La Cigale, a listed historic monument, and hosts musicals, rock and pop, and music festivals.

➕ c2 ✉ 120 boulevard Rochechouart, 75018 ☎ 01 49 25 89 99 🚇 Pigalle, Anvers

CAVEAU DE LA HUCHETTE
caveaudelahuchette.fr

Still going strong after 60 years, having regularly hosted all the great names in jazz, this atmospheric basement bar hosts live jazz and dancing.

➕ J7 ✉ 5 rue de la Huchette, 75005 ☎ 01 43 26 65 05 🕐 Daily from 9.30pm 🚇 Saint-Michel

LE CHAMPO
lechampo.com

Come here for cult classics, with retrospectives of directors such as the Marx Brothers, Claude Chabrol and Jacques Tati. Films are in the original language.

➕ J7 ✉ 51 rue des Écoles, 75015 ☎ 01 43 54 51 60 🕐 Daily, times vary 🚇 Saint-Michel, Odéon, Cluny–La Sorbonne

CLUB L'ARC
larc-paris.com

This long-standing favorite has been renovated by rock star Lenny Kravitz. It's now one of the most fashionable places in town and a hotspot for celebs.

➕ B2 ✉ 12 rue de Presbourg, 75016 ☎ 0659 21 32 44 🕐 Thu from 9.30 for women, midnight for men; Fri–Sat from midnight for both sexes 🚇 Charles de Gaulle–Étoile

COMÉDIE FRANÇAISE/ SALLE RICHELIEU
comedie-francaise.fr

The Comédie Française, home to France's most prestigious troupe of actors, was founded by Louis XIV in 1680. Today, the repertoire is made up of the classics, including works by Shakespeare, Molière and Victor Hugo, and a few modern pieces.

➕ G4 ✉ 1 place Colette, 75001 ☎ 01 44 58 14 00 🕐 Performances daily, times vary, some matinées Sat, Sun 🚇 Palais-Royal–Musée du Louvre

CONCRETE
concreteparis.fr

At the forefront in the resurgence of after-hours and all-day dance clubs, this large concrete space plays host to the latest sounds and DJ sets.

➕ M9 ✉ Port de la Rapée, 75012 ☎ 0628 52 00 18 🕐 Fri 9pm–7am, Sat 9pm–7am, Sun 7am–2am 🚇 Quai de la Gare

LE CRAZY HORSE
lecrazyhorseparis.com

This world-renowned burlesque show has been wowing audiences with its naughty but humorous routines, gorgeous dancers and dazzling, albeit scanty, costumes by top designers since 1951.

🔒 C4 ✉ 12 avenue George V 75008 ☎ 01 47 23 32 32 🕐 Shows: Sun–Fri 8.15 and 10.45, Sat 7, 9.30 and 11.45 🚇 George V, Alma–Marceau

DIVAN DU MONDE

divandumonde.com

The lower level of this former brothel is devoted to concerts of everything from rock to electronic and world music; the Divan Japonais upstairs holds themed evenings with DJs and video artists showing their talents.

🔒 C3 ✉ 75 rue des Martyrs, 75018 ☎ 01 40 05 06 99 🚇 Pigalle

DUC DES LOMBARDS

ducdeslombards.com

Prestigious jazz musicians regularly play in this Les Halles club. Late night Friday and Saturday there's free entry for a free-form jam session that carries on until the early hours.

🔒 J5 ✉ 42 rue des Lombards, 75001 ☎ 01 42 33 22 88 🕐 Closed Sun 🚇 Châtelet

FAVELA CHIC

favelachic.com

The sounds, flavors and vibrant style of urban Brazil ring out in this setting, with a restaurant, live bands and DJs. It includes a pop-up gallery and a chill-out lounge.

🔒 M3 ✉ 18 rue du Faubourg du Temple, 75011 ☎ 01 40 21 31 14 🕐 Tue–Sat 7.30pm–late 🚇 Pigalle

FORUM DES IMAGES

forumdesimages.fr

Films or documentaries shot in or connected with Paris and movie

classics are screened here, along with independent documentaries from around the world. A day pass admits you to all screenings. Visit the website for other venues around the city.

🔒 J5 ✉ 2 rue du Cinéma, Port Saint-Eustache, Forum des Halles, 75001 ☎ 01 44 76 63 00 🕐 Tue–Fri 1pm–9pm, Sat–Sun 2pm–9pm 🚇 Les Halles, Châtelet

HARRY'S NEW YORK BAR

harrys-bar.fr

Harry's in New York was dismantled and shipped lock, stock and barrel to Paris just before World War I. It's popular for its hundreds of cocktails.

🔒 G3 ✉ 5 rue Daunou, 75002 ☎ 01 42 61 71 14 🕐 Sun–Thu noon–2am, Fri–Sat noon–3am 🚇 Opéra

LUCERNAIRE/CENTRE NATIONAL D'ART ET D'ESSAI

lucernaire.fr

This complex of three cinemas, an art gallery, bar, restaurant and three theaters stages a wide variety of plays. Housed in a former factory, it attracts top French actors.

🔒 G8 ✉ 53 rue Notre-Dame-des-Champs, 75006 ☎ 01 45 44 57 34 🚇 Vavin, Notre-Dame-des-Champs

MICHOU

michou.fr

A familiar sight in the district, Michou is always dressed in electric-blue suits and big eye-glasses. The drag show in this venerable club is still going strong.

➕ c2 ✉ 80 rue des Martyrs, 75018
☎ 01 46 06 16 04 🕐 Nightly dinner 8.30, show 10.30 🚇 Pigalle

MOULIN ROUGE

moulinrouge.fr

The Red Windmill, made famous by Toulouse-Lautrec, opened in 1889 when audiences flocked to ogle at the dancers performing the cancan. These days the shows are still as spectacular but are more entertaining than scandalous.

➕ b2 ✉ 82 boulevard de Clichy, 75018
☎ 01 53 09 82 82 🕐 Nightly dinner and show 7pm; show only 9 and 11
🚇 Blanche

MUSÉE NATIONAL DU MOYEN-ÂGE

musee-moyenage.fr

This medieval mansion is home to a museum devoted to the Middle Ages (▷ 34–35), but it also hosts classical and chamber music concerts. Most appropriate are the concerts of medieval music

BEAUTIFUL PEOPLE

The clubs around the Champs-Élysées tend to attract VIPs, celebrities and a generally well-heeled crowd. Clubs usually don't open until 11pm or midnight, and often stay open until dawn. For a more laid-back, arty bar scene, go to the bar-lined rue Oberkampf or the Canal Saint-Martin area. The Marais district is also packed with bars, many of them gay or mixed.

in conjunction with the Centre de musique médiévale de Paris.

➕ J7 ✉ 6 place Paul-Painlevé, 75005
☎ 01 53 73 78 16 🕐 Free concerts of medieval music: times vary 🚇 Cluny–La Sorbonne

OPÉRA BASTILLE

operadeparis.fr

Paris's opera house towers over place de la Bastille and boasts five movable stages. The range of per-formances includes opera, operettas, recitals, ballet, dance and even theater.

➕ M7 ✉ 120 rue de Lyon, 75012
☎ 08 92 89 90 90 🚇 Bastille

PETIT JOURNAL MONTPARNASSE

petitjournalmontparnasse.com

This club, sister venue to the Petit Journal Saint-Michel, has hosted some of France's best-loved jazz musicians. You can dine while lis-tening or just have a drink.

➕ E9 ✉ 13 rue Commandant-Mouchotte, 75014 ☎ 01 43 21 56 70 🕐 Closed Sun and 3 weeks in summer
🚇 Montparnasse–Bienvenüe

PHILHARMONIE DE PARIS

philharmoniedeparis.fr

Inaugurated in 2015, the city's new, if controversial, 1,500-seat venue, is home to the Orchestre de Paris and offers a rich program of solo artists, classical and rock concerts, family events and music workshops.

➕ Off map at M1 ✉ 221 avenue Jean Jaurès, Parc de la Villette, 75019 ☎ 01 44 84 44 84 🚇 Porte de Pintin

QUEEN

queen.fr

This large club is still going strong and is popular with both straight and gay people. It hosts top DJs, with different themes each evening. The doormen are known to be very particular, so make sure you dress well.

🔲 C3 ✉ 79 avenue des Champs-Élysées, 75008 ☎ 01 53 89 08 90 ⏰ Daily midnight–7am (times can vary, some nights start earlier) 🚇 George V

STUDIO 28

cinema-studio28.com
Studio 28 is the coolest cinema in Paris, where new releases in the original language change every day or two, and French classics are screened every month. It has its own little bar and garden where you can mix with like-minded film aficionados.

🔲 b2 ✉ 10 rue Tholozé, 75018 ☎ 01 46 06 36 07 🚇 Abbesses, Blanche

STUDIO GALANDE

studiogalande.fr
Cult movie *The Rocky Horror Picture Show* is shown here every Friday and Saturday at 10pm. The rest of the week screenings vary from art films to cartoons.

🔲 J7 ✉ 42 rue Galande, 75005 ☎ 01 43 54 72 71 ⏰ Screenings daily from noon 🚇 Saint-Michel, Maubert–Mutualité, Cluny

SUNSET-SUNSIDE

sunset-sunside.com
Opened in 1984 as a venue for jazz of all descriptions, this club has evolved over the years into two jazz clubs: the Sunset offers a range of electric jazz and world music concerts, while the Sunside concentrates on acoustic jazz.

🔲 J5 ✉ 60 rue des Lombards, 75001 ☎ 01 40 26 46 60 ⏰ Live performances daily 8.30pm or 9pm 🚇 Châtelet

THÉÂTRE DU CHÂTELET

chatelet-theatre.com
The Théâtre du Châtelet hosts a varied schedule of opera, symphonic music and dance, as well as popular Sunday morning concerts. It seats 2,500 people.

🔲 J6 ✉ 2 rue Edouard Colonne, 75001 ☎ 01 40 28 28 40 ⏰ Check website calender 🚇 Châtelet

THÉÂTRE DE LA HUCHETTE

theatre-huchette.com
Two of Ionesco's masterpieces, *La Cantatrice Chauve* (The Bald Soprano) and *La Leçon* (The Lesson), have been performed here five days a week for over 50 years. It's an intimate venue with room for just 85 people.

🔲 J7 ✉ 23 rue de la Huchette, 75005 ☎ 01 43 26 38 99 ⏰ Tue–Sat 7pm and 8pm 🚇 Saint-Michel

THÉÂTRE DE LA VILLE

theatredelaville-paris.com
This modern venue showcases an adventurous program of avant-garde music, classical pieces, contemporary dance and plays, which include well-directed works by Shakespeare and Marlowe.

🔲 J6 ✉ 2 place du Châtelet, 75004 ☎ 01 42 74 22 77 ⏰ Performance times vary 🚇 Châtelet

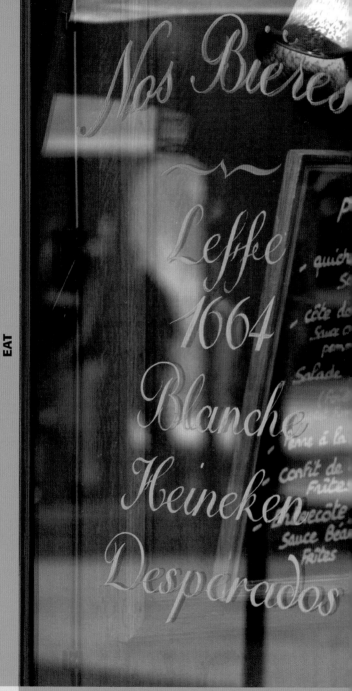

Eat

There are places to eat across the city to suit all tastes and budgets. In this section establishments are listed alphabetically.

EAT

Introduction

Paris is often described as the capital of gastronomy, so a meal out in the city has a lot to live up to. The standard for the best restaurants—the Michelin star—is famed throughout the world as the epitome of gastronomic excellence.

Budget Choices
If your budget isn't up to the crème-de-la-crème, there are hundreds of less expensive choices, from regional French cuisine to North African, Lebanese or Japanese.

The Very Best
Restaurants have higher prices than brasseries or bistros but will often provide a refined setting, elegant cuisine and a good wine list. For a special treat, look for multistarred Michelin chefs such as Alain Ducasse and Guy Savoy. Dress smartly and book in advance.

Lunch and Snacks
Cafés and bars serve coffee, tea, soft drinks, alcohol and snacks. Most open from around 9am (or earlier) until well into the evening and many have outdoor seating. *Salons de thé* (tearooms) open from noon until evening. If you are on a budget, have your main meal at lunchtime, when most restaurants serve a reasonably priced *menu du jour*, or daily menu, of two or three courses with a glass of wine.

OPENING TIMES

Most restaurants and bistros keep strict serving times. Restaurants open at 12, close at 2.30, then reopen at 7.30 or 8. Most Parisians take an hour for lunch and eat in the staff canteen or in a local bistro. The evening meal is the most important of the day and is usually taken *en famille* between 8 and 9pm. Restaurants stop taking orders between 10 and 11pm. To eat later, try the Les Halles area or a brasserie. Some places close on weekends and in July and August, and for holidays in February.

From top: wonderful views are to be had from Le Ciel de Paris; stopping for coffee; blackboard menu; a colorful dish at Guy Savoy's restaurant

Directory

Around the Tour Eiffel

Asian
Benkay
French-Bistro
L'Affriolé
Aux Enfants Gâtés
Bistrotrotters
French-Brasserie
Brasserie Thoumieux
French-Elegant
Le Ciel de Paris
Le Jules Verne
French-Regional
L'Ami Jean

Latin Quarter, St-Germain and Islands

Asian
Desi Road
French-Bistro
Le Comptoir
Les Papilles
Le Petit Saint-Benoît
Ze Kitchen Galerie
French-Brasserie
Alcazar
La Coupole
Le Petit Zinc
French-Elegant
Guy Savoy
La Tour d'Argent

Marais and Bastille

French-Bistro
L'Ange 20
Au Pied de Cochon
Bistrot Paul Bert
Chez Paul
Monjul
Pramil
French-Brasserie
Bofinger
French-Elegant
Le Dôme du Marais
French-Regional
Benoit

Kosher
L'As du Fallafel
North African
404

Louvre and Champs-Élysées

French-Bistro
Café Marly
Jean
Restaurant Frenchie
French-Elegant
Le Céladon
Epicure
Passage 53
Taillevent
French-Regional
Carré des Feuillants
Fusion
6 New York

Montmartre

French-Bistro
Au Virage Lepic
Le Progrès
Seb'on
French-Regional
Au Clair de la Lune
Organic
Rose Bakery

Farther Afield

French-Bistro
La Petite Ardoise
Septime
French-Elegant
Gordon Ramsay au Trianon

EAT

Eating A–Z

PRICES

Prices are approximate, based on a three-course meal for one person.

€€€	over €90
€€	€35–€90
€	under €35

6 NEW YORK €€

6newyork.fr

For beautiful contemporary decor and fusion food, head for 6 New York. Chef and owner Jerome Gangneux, who hails from Normandy, cooks with a lightness of touch that allows the fresh ingredients to reveal their flavors.

➕ B5 ✉ 6 avenue de New York, 75016 ☎ 01 40 70 03 30 ⏰ Mon–Fri lunch, dinner, Sat dinner 🚇 Alma–Marceau

404 €–€€

404-resto.com

This family-run restaurant serves excellent North African cuisine. Beautifully styled, it's like stepping into an Arab souk, with colorful ceramics, fine basketry and carpets festooned around. The dining room is part of an atmospheric 16th-century stone building.

➕ K4 ✉ 69 rue des Gravilliers, 75003 ☎ 01 42 74 57 81 ⏰ Daily lunch, dinner 🚇 Arts et Métiers

L'AFFRIOLÉ €€

laffriole.fr

This great value nouveau bistro provides friendly service and classic French dishes with a twist. All wines are available by the glass, which is rare in Paris.

➕ C5 ✉ 17 rue Malar, 75007 ☎ 01 44 18 31 33 ⏰ Tue–Sat lunch, dinner 🚇 La Tour Maubourg, Pont de l'Alma, Invalides

ALCAZAR €€

alcazar.fr

Reopened after a total renovation, Alcazar has emerged with rein-vented decor and a new menu. Michel Besmond oversees a selection of fresh and adventurous dishes, served in the eclectically styled yet relaxed dining room.

➕ H6 ✉ 62 rue Mazarine, 75006 ☎ 01 53 10 19 99 ⏰ Daily lunch, dinner 🚇 Odéon

Coffees and beers in the Marais district

L'AMI JEAN €€

lamijean.fr

Owned by chef Stéphane Jego, an apprentice of pioneer Yves Camdeborde, this friendly restaurant serves traditional Basque dishes of beef and seafood, given a contemporary twist and enhanced by fine wines.

⊞ C5 ⊠ 27 rue Malar, 75007 ☎ 01 47 05 86 89 🕐 Tue–Sat lunch, dinner 🚇 Pont de l'Alma, La Tour Maubourg, Invalides

L'ANGE 20 €€

lange20.com

The L'Ange 20 team were so successful, they moved to bigger premises in 2015. They keep their menu very simple, with typically Parisian fare. It is still an intimate space despite being larger than their old venue.

⊞ K5 ⊠ 44 rue des Tournelles, 75004 ☎ 01 49 96 58 39 🕐 Wed–Sun lunch, dinner 🚇 Bastille

L'AS DU FALLAFEL €

This kosher restaurant has a cult following among visitors and Marais locals alike for its falafel and low prices. An advantage here is that you can eat in or take out. Expect to wait in line but it will be worth it.

⊞ L6 ⊠ 34 rue des Rosiers, 75007 ☎ 01 48 87 63 60 🕐 Sun–Thu 12–12, Fri lunch only 🚇 Saint-Paul

AU CLAIR DE LA LUNE €€

Classic French cuisine is served in this comfortable, welcoming inn-style restaurant just off the place du Tertre. It is run by two brothers and is popular with locals.

⊞ c1 ⊠ 9 rue Poulbot, 75018 ☎ 01 42 58 97 03 🕐 Daily lunch, dinner 🚇 Abbesses

AU PIED DE COCHON €€

pieddecochon.com

Pigs' trotters feature at this Parisian institution, along with seafood and sublime French onion soup, served in elegant surroundings. It's extremely popular with the late-night set, and sees crowds of Parisians and tourists alike.

⊞ J4 ⊠ 6 rue Coquillère, 75001 ☎ 01 40 13 77 00 🕐 Daily 24 hours 🚇 Les Halles

AU VIRAGE LEPIC €–€€

This welcoming bistro is well known for its tasty meat-based main courses and delicious puddings, complemented by a great wine list. In summer you can sit outside.

⊞ b1 ⊠ 61 rue Lepic, 75018 ☎ 01 42 52 46 79 🕐 Wed–Mon dinner 🚇 Blanche, Abbesses

AUX ENFANTS GÂTÉS €€

auxenfantsgates.fr

Frédéric Bidault's small modern eatery offers a limited daily menu of classic French bistro dishes including *pâté en croûte* (pâté in pastry case) and *jarret de veau* (veal shank).

⊞ Off map ⊠ 4 rue Danville, 75014 ☎ 01 40 47 56 81 🕐 Tue–Sat lunch, dinner 🚇 Denfert Rochereau

BENKAY €€

restaurant-benkay.com

Dine here on modern Japanese food with panoramic views from the fourth floor of the Novotel Paris Tour Eiffel. Choose from a full-service sushi bar, a *washoku* traditional Japanese menu, and a showy *teppanyaki* station.

⊞ A7 ⊠ 61 quai de Grenelle, 75015 ☎ 01 40 58 21 26 🕐 Daily lunch, dinner 🚇 Bir-Hakeim

BENOIT €€–€€€

benoit-paris.com

This long-standing award-winning bistro serving classic regional dishes is owned by renowned chef Alain Ducasse. The dining room has an elegant period interior, matched by the fine food that is beautifully served by knowledgeable staff. Reserve ahead.

🚇 J6 ✉ 20 rue Saint-Martin, 75004 ☎ 01 58 00 22 05 🕐 Daily lunch, dinner 🚇 Hôtel de Ville, Châtelet-Les Halles

BISTROT PAUL BERT €€

One of the last old-style bistros, Bistrot Paul Bert has a loyal clientele that comes back again and again for generous portions, the best steak in town, and a cheese plate that takes you on a dairy tour of France. The soufflés are pretty good too.

🚇 Off map ✉ 18 rue Paul Bert 75011 🕐 01 43 72 24 01 🕐 Tue–Sat lunch, dinner 🚇 Faidherbe–Chaligny, rue des Boulets

BISTROTTERS €€

bistrotters.com

A small culinary team brings the flavors of the world to French ingredients in a pretty bistro setting in the Montparnasse area. There's a wine shop on site where you can stock up on the bottles you enjoyed over dinner.

🚇 Off map ✉ 9 rue Decrès, 75014 ☎ 01 45 45 58 59 🕐 Tue–Sat lunch, dinner 🚇 Plaisance

BOFINGER €€

bofingerparis.com

Claiming to be the oldest brasserie in Paris (1864), Bofinger adheres strongly to the traditional brasserie menu and serves seafood, choucroute and steaks, plus the ubiquitous onion soup. The elegant interior is period-perfect art nouveau in style.

🚇 M6 ✉ 5 rue de la Bastille, 75004 ☎ 01 42 72 87 82 🕐 Daily lunch, dinner 🚇 Bastille

BRASSERIE THOUMIEUX €€

thoumieux.com

Established in 1923, the elegant dining room has velvet wall seats and is decorated with lots of mirrors. Expect hearty cassoulet (sausage and bean casserole) or duck dishes. Upstairs is the pricey fine dining Restaurant Sylvestre.

🚇 D5 ✉ 79 rue Saint-Dominique, 75007 ☎ 01 47 05 79 00 🕐 Daily lunch, dinner 🚇 Invalides

CAFÉ MARLY €€

cafe-marly.com

This classy café-restaurant located in the Louvre must have one of the best terraces in the world, with its exceptional view of architect I.M. Pei's stunning glass pyramid and the opposite wing of the museum behind it. The food is reliably good and the service is friendly.

🚇 G5 ✉ 93 rue de Rivoli, 75001 ☎ 01 49 26 06 60 🕐 Daily 8am–2am (last orders midnight) 🚇 Palais-Royal–Musée du Louvre

CARRÉ DES FEUILLANTS €€€

carredesfeuillants.fr

You'll find an elegant setting for Alain Dutournier's brilliant evocation of the cooking of his native Gascony. He uses the best ingredients to wonderful effect, earning a high reputation for his restaurant.

🚇 F4 ✉ 14 rue de Castiglione, 75001 ☎ 01 42 86 82 82 🕐 Mon–Fri lunch, dinner, Sat dinner. Closed Aug 🚇 Tuileries

The French are famous for their crusty bread

LE CÉLADON €€–€€€

leceladon.com

Serving interesting variations on French classics, Le Céladon offers a good-value weekday lunch menu ideal for those who want to begin to explore French haute-cuisine. It opens as Le Petit Céladon on weekends.

➕ G3 ✉ Hotel Westminster, 15 rue Daunou, 75002 ☎ 01 47 03 40 42 ⏰ Mon–Fri lunch, dinner. Closed Aug 🚇 Opéra

CHEZ PAUL €–€€

chezpaul.com

This authentic Paris bistro serves staples such as *escargots* (snails) and *soupe à l'oignon* (onion soup) at reasonable prices. Just like the menu, the decor hasn't been changed in decades, which makes it all the more fun.

➕ Off map ✉ 13 rue de Charonne 75011 ☎ 01 47 00 34 57 ⏰ Daily lunch, dinner 🚇 Bastille, Ledru Rollin

LE CIEL DE PARIS €€–€€€

cieldeparis.com

Whizz your way up to the 56th floor of the Tour Montparnasse, to the highest restaurant in Paris. The changing menu may include pan-sautéed fillet of beef with a

truffle sauce, lobster risotto, or fried scallops with a parsley purée.

➕ F9 ✉ Tour Montparnasse, 33 avenue du Maine, 75015 ☎ 01 40 64 77 64 ⏰ Daily breakfast, lunch, dinner 🚇 Montparnasse–Bienvenüe

LE COMPTOIR €€

hotel-paris-relais-saint-germain.com

This gastro-bistro, under the expert eye of chef Yves Camdeborde, champions modern French cuisine. Reservations are not taken for lunch, but it's best to reserve ahead for dinner.

➕ H7 ✉ Hôtel Relais Saint-Germain, 9 carrefour de l'Odéon, 75006 ☎ 01 44 27 07 97 ⏰ Daily lunch, dinner 🚇 Odéon

LA COUPOLE €€

lacoupole-paris.com

This Montparnasse brasserie offers reasonably priced set menus plus

EAT

all the standard dishes, but the elegant art deco setting and buzzy ambience are what make it memorable.

🔲 F9 ✉ 102 boulevard du Montparnasse, 75014 ☎ 01 43 20 14 20 🕐 Daily lunch, dinner 🚇 Vavin

DESI ROAD €€

desiroadrestaurant.com

One of the city's best Indian restaurants, with beautiful decor and attentive service, Desi Road serves a range of traditional curries.

🔲 H6 ✉ 14 rue Dauphine, 75006 ☎ 01 43 26 44 91 🕐 Tue–Sun lunch, dinner 🚇 Pont Neuf, Odéon

LE DÔME DU MARAIS €€

ledomedumarais.fr

Seasonal produce meets creative modern touches in dishes that

Delectable oysters

combine European and Southeast Asian ingredients at this restaurant in the rotunda of a former credit union. It's also a tea room in the afternoon.

🔲 L5 ✉ 53 bis rue des Francs-Bourgeois, 75004 ☎ 01 42 74 54 17 🕐 Wed–Thu dinner, Fri–Sun lunch, dinner 🚇 Hôtel de Ville, Rambuteau, Saint-Paul

EPICURE €€€

lebristolparis.com

Eric Frechon's superb restaurant offers the epitome of French gastronomic dining within the magnificent Bristol Hotel. Expect an inventive menu to titillate the taste buds. The hotel's attractive gardens make a wonderful place for an alfresco dinner during the summer.

🔲 D3 ✉ 112 rue du Faubourg Saint Honoré, 75008 ☎ 01 53 43 43 00 🕐 Daily breakfast, lunch, dinner 🚇 Saint-Philippe du Roule

GORDON RAMSAY AU TRIANON €€€

gordonramsay.com

Round off a day of splendor in Versailles with a sumptuous dinner in Gordon Ramsay's much-praised dining room in the Trianon Palace Hotel, where the menu makes lavish use of luxurious ingredients such as lobster and foie gras.

🔲 Off map ✉ 1 boulevard de la Reine, 78000, Versailles ☎ 01 30 84 55 55 🕐 Tue–Thu dinner, Fri–Sat lunch, dinner,

EAT

NEW BISTROS

Paris may be the food capital of the world, with more than its share of top restaurants, but not everyone can afford the astronomical prices of the best eateries. Some 15 years ago a few famous chefs opened "baby bistros," which benefited from their expertise but offered fine meals in often nondescript surroundings for reasonable prices. The trend has now expanded and Paris is full of nouveaux bistros.

Sun lunch 🚆 SNCF Versailles Rive Droite or RER Versailles Rive Gauche

GUY SAVOY €€€

guysavoy.com

At this gastronomic temple, in a stunning new home at the renovated La Monnaie de Paris (Paris Mint building), chef Guy Savoy makes cooking an art form. It is expensive, of course, but certainly exquisite; expect an unforgettable dining experience.

➕ H6 ✉ Monnaie de Paris, 11 quai de Conti, 75006 🕐 Tue–Fri lunch, dinner, Sat dinner 🚇 Pont Neuf

JEAN €€–€€€

restaurantjean.fr

Discover comfort food at this award-winning restaurant with dishes by Jean-Frédéric Guidoni that meld French ingredients with hints of the Caribbean and Asia.

➕ H2 ✉ 8 rue Saint-Lazare, 75009 ☎ 01 48 78 62 73 🕐 Tue–Sat lunch, dinner. Closed Aug 🚇 Notre-Dame-de-Lorette, Trinité

LE JULES VERNE €€€

lejulesverne-paris.com

Alain Ducasse's wonderful restaurant, located on level two of the Eiffel Tower, is the talk of Paris with its superb food and spectacular views over the city. Reservations are essential.

➕ B6 ✉ 2nd level, Tour Eiffel, 75007 (private elevator) ☎ 01 45 55 61 44 🕐 Daily lunch, dinner 🚇 Bir-Hakeim

MONJUL €€

monjul.com

One of a new generation of experimental chefs, the talented Julien Agobert produces inventive dishes that are works of art, and taste as

good as they look. There's liberal use of edible flowers to give the dishes a picturesque quality.

➕ K5 ✉ 28 rue des Blancs Manteaux, 75004 ☎ 01 42 74 40 15 🕐 Tue–Sat lunch, dinner 🚇 Rambuteau

LES PAPILLES €–€€

lespapillesparis.fr

The authentic decor sets you up for a genuine bistro experience where you can choose from a daily set menu of French dishes made with market-fresh ingredients. There's also a wine and fine food store.

➕ H8 ✉ 30 rue Gay-Lussac 75005 ☎ 01 43 25 20 79 🕐 Tue-Sat 12–2, 7–10.30 🚇 RER Luxembourg

PASSAGE 53 €€–€€€

passage53.com

Shinishi Sato's tiny restaurant in Paris's oldest shopping arcade packs a culinary punch, combining French ingredients with a modern approach. Sato is the first Japanese chef in France to earn two Michelin stars. Reservation is recommended.

➕ H3 ✉ 53 Passage des Panoramas, 75002 ☎ 01 42 33 04 35 🕐 Tue–Sat lunch, dinner 🚇 Grands Boulevards

LE PETIT SAINT-BENOÎT €

petit-st-benoit.com

This popular, inexpensive classic was once the haunt of writers; the

EAT

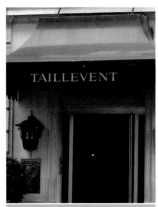

Taillevent is renowned for good food

decor has barely changed since the 1930s. The menu features a long list of French classics ranging from frogs legs to boeuf bourguignon.

➕ G6 ✉ 4 rue Saint-Benoît, 75006 ☎ 01 42 60 27 92 🕐 Mon–Sat lunch, dinner 🚇 Saint-Germain-des-Prés

LE PETIT ZINC €€

petit-zinc.com

There's a classic Belle Époque interior in this brasserie, which concentrates on seafood and serves inspiring dishes such as sea bass cooked in an earthenware brick or mouthwatering Grand Marnier soufflé.

➕ G6 ✉ 11 rue Saint-Benoît, 75006 ☎ 01 42 86 61 00 🕐 Daily 12–12 🚇 Saint-Germain-des-Prés

LA PETITE ARDOISE €–€€

restaurantlapetiteardoise.fr

Regarded as one of the most popular restaurants in Fontainebleau, La Petite Ardoise serves classic French dishes from a variety of regions in France. Diners can choose either small plates or large plates depending on their appetite.

➕ Off map ✉ 16 rue Montebello, 77300 Fontainebleau ☎ 01 64 24 08 66 🕐 Tue–Sat lunch, dinner 🚇 Fontainebleau–Avon

PRAMIL €–€€

pramil.fr

With a menu based on seasonal produce, Alain Pramil has built up a loyal customer base. The presentation is refined and all at prices that make this one of Paris's best bistros in this price range.

➕ L4 ✉ 9 rue du Vertbois ☎ 01 42 72 03 60 🕐 Tue–Sat lunch, dinner, Sun dinner 🚇 Arts et Métiers, Temple

LE PROGRÈS €–€€

This is the kind of café where you'd expect to see a character from the 2001 film *Amélie*, which was shot in the area. The staff provide expert service and the *plat du jour* always draws in the lunchtime crowds.

➕ c2 ✉ 7 rue des Trois-Frères, 75018 ☎ 01 42 64 07 37 🕐 Daily 9am–2am 🚇 Abbesses

RESTAURANT FRENCHIE €€

frenchie-restaurant.com

This, one of the best nouveau bistros in the city, is owned by Gregory Marchand, who worked with Jamie Oliver in London before returning to his native France. The menu is limited but the fusion dishes are superb. The only downside is that you'll need to reserve at least a month ahead to be sure of getting a table. Try Marchand's wine bar across the street if Frenchie is full.

➕ J4 ✉ 5–6 rue du Nil, 75002 ☎ 01 40 39 96 10 🕐 Mon–Fri dinner, reservations obligatory 🚇 Sentier

ROSE BAKERY €–€€

Organic food is served in this English bakery and tea shop, owned by a Franco-British couple. It is also a popular place for Sunday brunch.

🔢 c3 ✉ 46 rue des Martyrs, 75009 ☎ 01 42 82 12 80 🕐 Daily 9–6 (menu items 11–5.30) 🚇 Pigalle, Notre-Dame-de-Lorette

SEB'ON €€

seb-on.com

One of the best of a collection of modern bistros that have sprung up in the Montmartre area, Seb'on is a tiny, intimate place with a kitchen presided over by Sebastien Heloin. He serves a small and ever-changing daily menu of market-fresh dishes with suitably impressive results.

🔢 H1 ✉ 62 rue d'Orsel, 75018 ☎ 01 42 59 74 32 🕐 Sat–Sun lunch, Wed–Sat dinner 🚇 Abbesses

SEPTIME €€

septime-charonne.fr

One of a new generation of fine dining restaurants in Paris, Septime has quickly built legions of loyal patrons, though you'll have to surrender yourself to chef Bertrand Grebaut's fixed menu for dinner (you'll be asked about any food allergies before you are served). The value lunch offers a choice of options.

🔢 Off map ✉ 80 rue de Charonne, 75011 ☎ 01 43 67 38 29 🕐 Mon dinner, Tue–Fri lunch, dinner 🚇 Charonne

TAILLEVENT €€€

taillevent.com

The cooking has classical foundations with subtle modern leanings at this discreetly elegant restaurant. Opened in 1950, it steadily gained in popularity and is worthy of its excellent reputation.

🔢 C2 ✉ 15 rue Lamennais, 75008 ☎ 01 44 95 15 01 🕐 Mon–Fri lunch, dinner. Closed late Jul to mid-Aug 🚇 George V, Charles de Gaulle–Étoile

LA TOUR D'ARGENT €€€

latourdargent.com

Come to this historic fine dining restaurant in the Latin Quarter for its fabulous view, its great wine cellar and the tasty duck. It is superb.

🔢 K7 ✉ 15–17 quai de la Tournelle, 75005 (facing Île Saint-Louis) ☎ 01 43 54 23 31 🕐 Tue–Sat lunch, dinner. Closed Aug 🚇 Pont-Marie, Cardinal Lemoine

ZE KITCHEN GALERIE €€

zekitchengalerie.fr

Inventive cuisine rewarded by a Michelin star shines out at this chic restaurant. Chef William Ledeuil artfully combines the tastes and textures of southeast Asia with French techniques to produce creative dishes. The seasonal menu has fresh ingredients supplied by a select team of French growers.

🔢 H6 ✉ 4 rue des Grands-Augustins, 75006 ☎ 01 44 32 00 32 🕐 Mon–Fri lunch, dinner 🚇 Odéon

> ### PICNIC LUNCHES
>
> If your taste is for a *déjeuner sur l'herbe* in Fontainebleau, the rue Grande grocery stores are perfect for picnic supplies. In Versailles, the Marché Notre-Dame is an excellent covered market (closed on Mondays) for stocking up on lunch items. When in Chantilly, allow yourself to be tempted by the bakeries, with their delicious cakes and pastries, with lashings of the eponymous cream.

Sleep

With options ranging from the luxurious to simple budget hotels, Paris has accommodations to suit everyone. In this section establishments are listed alphabetically.

SLEEP

Introduction

The city's hotels have seen an overhaul in recent years. Boutique hotels have sprung up all over Paris, especially in the Marais. Hotels around the Louvre, Champs-Élysées and Opéra tend to be more expensive, while those in the Latin Quarter are often smaller and more affordable.

Finding a Good Deal

Some of the luxury hotels are out of another era. Their stated prices are high but discounts can be found online or through some travel agents. Paris is one of the rare European capitals where you can find a pleasant, affordable place to stay in a central part of the city. The Paris Tourist Office (▷ 167) has information. You can reserve rooms if you visit in person.

Helpful Tips

Prices often drop in July and August and rise in May, June, September and October, for the trade fairs. Check whether the price includes breakfast. If you are bringing or renting a car, ask whether parking is available and the cost.

Outer Limits

Chain hotels on the outskirts can be less expensive, but they lack character. You'll also have to spend more time taking the Métro.

APARTMENT LIVING

● To rent an apartment, options include the UK-based Apartment Service (tel 020 8944 1444 from the UK; 011 44 20 8944 1444 from the US, apartmentservice.com) and Home Rental Service at 120 avenue des Champs-Élysées, 75008 (tel 01 42 25 65 40, homerental.fr).
● For bed-and-breakfast try France Lodge at 2 rue Meissonnier, 75017 (tel 01 56 33 85 80, francelodge.fr); Good Morning Paris, 43 rue Lacépède, 75005 (tel 01 47 07 28 29, goodmorningparis.fr); and Bed & Breakfast France, Bellenuoe, 85180 Château D'Olonne (tel 09 60 09 86 49, bedbreak.com).

From top: an elegant entrance; the lobby of Le Meurice; let someone else take the strain with your luggage; a junior suite at Le Meurice

Directory

Around the Tour Eiffel

Budget
Hôtel de l'Avre
Hôtel Eiffel Turenne

Latin Quarter, St-Germain and Islands

Budget
Hôtel du Collège de France
Mid-Range
The Five Hotel
Hôtel d'Angleterre
Hôtel Design de la Sorbonne
Hôtel Duc de Saint-Simon
Hôtel des Marronniers
Hôtel La Perle
Hôtel Sainte-Beuve
Hôtel de l'Université
Les Rives de Notre-Dame
Luxury
L'Hôtel
Hôtel du Jeu de Paume
Hôtel de l'Abbaye

Marais and Bastille

Budget
Grand Hôtel Malher

Hôtel de la Place des Vosges
Luxury
1K
Pavillon de la Reine

Louvre and Champs-Élysées

Mid-Range
Hôtel Lautrec Opéra
Hôtel Molière
Hotel Résidence Foch
Résidence Lord Byron
Luxury
Hôtel San Régis
Le Meurice

Montmartre

Budget
Hôtel 29 Lepic
Timhotel Montmartre

Sleeping A–Z

PRICES

Prices are approximate and based on a double room for one night.

€€€	€251–€800
€€	€151–€250
€	€50–€150

1K €€€

1K-paris.com
Sharp modern design, variable lighting effects and great attention to detail characterize this boutique hotel. There are 43 rooms and 9 suites (some have an interior courtyard view), a highly popular bar, covered terrace, and in-house restaurant.

⊞ M4 ✉ 13 boulevard du Temple, 75003 ☎ 01 42 71 20 00 🚇 Filles du Calvaire

THE FIVE HOTEL €€–€€€

thefivehotel.com
Luxurious touches, such as L'Occitane toiletries, point to a standard of quality at this boutique hotel. There's no doubt that the rooms here are tiny but what they

lack in space, they make up for in style, with their clean lines and blocks of color.

🔲 J9 ✉ 3 rue Flatters, 75005 ☎ 01 43 31 73 21 🚇 Gobelins

GRAND HÔTEL MALHER €–€€

grandhotelmalher.com

A longstanding Paris hotel, Grand Hôtel Malher has reinvented itself with a contemporary makeover but it continues to be reasonably priced for its central location. The quieter rooms look out over a pretty rear courtyard.

🔲 L6 ✉ 5 rue Malher, 75004 ☎ 01 42 72 60 92 🚇 Saint-Paul

L'HÔTEL €€€

l-hotel.com

L'Hôtel is a Parisian legend that is exuberantly elegant and intimate. Oscar Wilde stayed here and celebrities can often be found in the discreet bar. There are 20 individually styled rooms, some superbly appointed, as well as a hammam pool where guests can relax, and a restaurant.

🔲 G6 ✉ 13 rue des Beaux-Arts, 75006 ☎ 01 44 41 99 00 🚇 Saint-Germain-des-Prés

---

BUDGET HOTELS

Gone are the heady days when Paris was peppered with atmospheric basic hotels with their inimitable signs "eau à tous les étages" (water on every floor). Now there are usually bath or shower rooms with every bedroom, resulting in higher prices and smaller rooms.

So don't expect much space in budget hotel rooms, and be aware that breakfast may not be included. Receptionists usually speak a second language in hotels with two or more stars.

HÔTEL 29 LEPIC €€

29lepic.fr

This three-star hotel is near the Sacré-Cœur. Its simple but bright bedrooms have been carefully furnished. There's free WiFi throughout and generous breakfast hours of 7am until 11am.

🔲 b2 ✉ 29 rue Lepic, 75018 ☎ 01 56 55 50 04 🚇 Blanche, Abbesses

HÔTEL DE L'ABBAYE €€€

hotel-abbaye.com

This quaint, historic hotel was once a convent and now has a country house atmosphere. The lounge and most of the 40 rooms overlook a patio which makes a great place to relax. There's a cozy bar on site.

🔲 G7 ✉ 10 rue Cassette, 75006 ☎ 01 45 44 38 11 🚇 Saint-Sulpice

HÔTEL D'ANGLETERRE €€

hotel-dangleterre.com

This former 18th-century British embassy has a garden patio and individually appointed spacious rooms with an elegant period feel. Ernest Hemingway lived in room 14 in 1921. There is a bar and a relaxing piano lounge.

🔲 G6 ✉ 44 rue Jacob, 75006 ☎ 01 42 60 34 72 🚇 Saint-Germain-des-Prés

HÔTEL DE L'AVRE €

hoteldelavre.com

This impeccably kept two-star hotel is justifiably popular with guests. The 25 rooms are individually decorated, vary in size and some look out over the rear courtyard. Breakfast is served in the pretty garden in spring and summer.

🔲 B8 ✉ 21 rue de l'Avre, 75015 ☎ 01 45 75 31 03 🚇 La Motte-Picquet–Grenelle

HÔTEL DU COLLÈGE DE FRANCE €–€€

hotel-collegedefrance.com

This inexpensive family-owned hotel is set behind a Haussman-designed facade. There are 29 well-presented simple but modern rooms that vary in size. All are en suite; some have small balconies overlooking the street.

✠ J7 ✉ 7 rue Thénard, 75005 ☎ 01 43 26 78 36 Ⓜ Maubert–Mutualité

HÔTEL DESIGN DE LA SORBONNE €–€€

hotelsorbonne.com

This hotel has contemporary living down to a fine art. Each floor has photos, engravings and literary quotes that complement the British-style decor. The 38 bedrooms have iMac computers, among the lavish facilities.

✠ H8 ✉ 6 rue Victor-Cousin, 75005 ☎ 01 43 54 58 08 Ⓜ Cluny–La Sorbonne

HÔTEL DUC DE SAINT-SIMON €€

hotelducdesaintsimon.com

This elegant 18th-century townhouse has been transformed into a sumptuous small hotel with delightful period styling. Rather pricey (at the top end of mid-range) but the antiques and setting, just off boulevard Saint-Germain, justify it. There are 34 comfortable rooms.

✠ F6 ✉ 14 rue Saint-Simon, 75007 ☎ 01 44 39 20 20 Ⓜ Rue du Bac

HOTEL EIFFEL TURENNE €€

hoteleiffelturenne.com

The bright and cozy rooms of this two-star hotel are comfortably furnished, though don't expect anything very spacious. Some rooms have views of the Eiffel Tower, which is only a short stroll away through the Champ de Mars. There's a small bar on site.

✠ D6 ✉ 20 avenue de Tourville, 75007 ☎ 01 47 05 99 92 Ⓜ École Militaire

HÔTEL DU JEU DE PAUME €€€

jeudepaumehotel.com

This small, delightful hotel is carved out of a 17th-century royal tennis court. The interior is a surprise considering the age of the buildings, with many contemporary touches. There are 27 tasteful rooms and two large apartments for longer rentals.

✠ K7 ✉ 54 rue Saint-Louis-en-l'Île, 75004 ☎ 01 43 26 14 18 Ⓜ Pont Marie

HÔTEL LAUTREC OPÉRA €–€€

paris-hotel-lautrec.com

This three-star hotel is named after the artist Henri Toulouse-Lautrec, who once lived here, and is classified a historic monument. Inside, there's a more contemporary feel, with pale wood furniture and blue-and-yellow upholstery. Some rooms have exposed bricks and beams but with 21st-century equipment such as satellite TV.

✠ H3 ✉ 8–10 rue d'Amboise, 75002 ☎ 01 42 96 67 90 Ⓜ Richelieu–Drouot

HÔTEL DES MARRONNIERS €€

hoteldesmarronniers.com

The oak-beamed rooms and vaulted cellars here have been converted to relaxing lounges. There are 37 well-appointed and comfortable rooms; ask for one overlooking the garden, a wonderful addition to a city hotel, which houses a *salon du thé*.

✠ G6 ✉ 21 rue Jacob, 75006 ☎ 01 43 25 30 60 Ⓜ Saint-Germain-des-Prés

HÔTEL MOLIÈRE €€

hotel-moliere.fr

One of the city's newest boutique hotels, the Molière has been renovated and revamped to offer calm zen-like interiors. There are 32 rooms, one with a good-sized balcony. There's a sauna/wellness/fitness center on site, but no restaurant.

➕ G4 ✉ 21 rue Molière, 75001 ☎ 01 42 96 22 01 🚇 Pyramides, Palais-Royal

HÔTEL LA PERLE €€

hotel-paris-laperle.com

This renovated 17th-century building on a quiet street has 38 rooms. It lies at the upper end of the mid-range price bracket, but the attention to detail, room decor and spacious communal areas are worth it. The large veranda is a charming setting for drinks. There's also a fitness room.

➕ G7 ✉ 14 rue des Canettes, 75006 ☎ 01 43 29 10 10 🚇 Mabillon

HÔTEL DE LA PLACE DES VOSGES €

hotelplacedesvosges.com

Located on a quiet street, this 17th-century town house in the Marais offers minimalist styling, mixing period furniture and architectural details with stark white

---

LE CRILLON

Whether you stay at the Ritz, the Crillon, the Meurice, the Bristol or the Georges V, they all have their tales to tell, but that of the Crillon (currently undergoing renovation) is perhaps the most momentous. This mansion managed to survive the Revolution despite having the guillotine on its doorstep. Mary Pickford and Douglas Fairbanks spent their honeymoon here.

---

walls. Some of the 16 rooms overlook the courtyard.

➕ M6 ✉ 12 rue de Birague, 75004 ☎ 01 42 72 60 46 🚇 Bastille, Saint-Paul

HOTEL RÉSIDENCE FOCH €–€€

foch-paris-hotel.com

This three-star hotel has a range of elegantly furnished rooms filled with quality furniture and traditional touches. Some rooms have balconies or small terraces. There's a bar on the ground floor and a courtyard garden.

➕ Off map at A3 ✉ 10 rue Marbeau, 75016 ☎ 01 45 00 46 50 🚇 Porte Dauphine

HÔTEL SAINTE-BEUVE €€–€€€

hotelsaintebeuve.com

Between Montparnasse and the Luxembourg gardens, this exclusive hotel features a stylish blend of period antiques and modern furnishings. It has the atmosphere of a private club. Standard rooms are small, but there are connecting rooms to cater to families.

➕ G8 ✉ 9 rue Sainte-Beuve, 75006 ☎ 01 45 48 20 07 🚇 Notre-Dame-des-Champs

HÔTEL SAN RÉGIS €€€

hotel-sanregis.fr

Popular with showbiz folk, this elaborately decorated hotel has 32 rooms and 11 suites. Interior designer Pierre-Yves Rochon mixes antique pieces with ornate chintz to recreate classic French Empire style in its elegant interiors. It's certainly exclusive, with prices to match.

➕ D4 ✉ 12 rue Jean-Goujon, 75008 ☎ 01 44 95 16 16 🚇 Franklin D. Roosevelt, Champs-Élysées–Clémenceau

Mid-priced establishments are popular with business visitors, so it is virtually impossible to find rooms during the trade-fair seasons (May to early June and mid-September to October). In summer many offer discounts as their clientele shrinks. All rooms are equipped with TV, phone, private bath or shower rooms and minibar, and most supply a hairdryer. Air-conditioning is not standard, but elevators are common.

HÔTEL DE L'UNIVERSITÉ €€

universitehotel.com

This Left Bank hotel *par excellence* has 27 rooms, some with (non-working) fireplaces, antique furnishings and exposed beams. The soothing pastel decor in the rooms and communal areas offers a calming refuge from city hustle and bustle after busy days of sightseeing.

➕ G6 ✉ 22 rue de l'Université, 75007 ☎ 01 42 61 09 39 🚇 Rue du Bac

LE MEURICE €€€

dorchestercollection.com

Situated just across the street from the Louvre, this historic 18th-century hotel has been thoroughly modernized, but the luxurious furnishings in the 160 rooms have more than a touch of Louis XVI style about them. French master-chef Alain Ducasse stamps his inimitable mark on the dining.

➕ F5 ✉ 228 rue de Rivoli, 75001 ☎ 01 44 58 10 10 🚇 Concorde, Tuileries

PAVILLON DE LA REINE €€€

pavillon-de-la-reine.com

Period decoration and lavish furnishings in this 17th-century building are enhanced by the leafy garden. There are 54 rooms and suites. The hotel has a small spa but no restaurant.

➕ M6 ✉ 28 place des Vosges, 75003 ☎ 01 40 29 19 19 🚇 Bastille, Chemin Vert

RÉSIDENCE LORD BYRON €–€€

hotel-lordbyron.fr

This inexpensive three-star city-center hotel benefits from a shady interior garden for alfresco breakfast or relaxing on warm summer evenings. The en suite rooms are an ample size; some overlook the attractive garden.

➕ C2 ✉ 5 rue Châteaubriand, 75008 ☎ 01 43 59 89 98 🚇 Georges V

LES RIVES DE NOTRE-DAME €€–€€€

rivesdenotredame.com

Overlooking the banks of the Seine, this hotel has beamed ceilings, marble tiling, tapestries and fine wrought-iron furniture. It's a small property of only 10 rooms, so you are guaranteed an intimate atmosphere and a warm welcome. There are views of the river and Notre Dame from some rooms.

➕ J7 ✉ 15 quai Saint-Michel, 75005 ☎ 01 43 54 81 16 🚇 Saint-Michel

TIMHOTEL MONTMARTRE €–€€

timhotel.com

On the tree-shaded place Émile Goudeau, this charming and popular hotel set behind a period facade has the rare advantage of panoramic views of Paris from some rooms.

➕ b2 ✉ 11 rue Ravignan, 75018 ☎ 01 42 55 74 79 🚇 Abbesses

SLEEP

Need to Know

This section takes you through all the practical aspects of your trip to make it run more smoothly and to give you confidence before you go and while you are there.

Planning Ahead

WHEN TO GO

Spring is a popular time, with its lovely chestnut blossoms. The city reaches peak tourist capacity in hot, sunny July. However, with the Parisian exodus to the countryside in August the city is emptier than usual. Autumn is busy with trade fairs and rooms can be scarce and expensive.

TIME

Paris is one hour ahead of London, six hours ahead of New York and nine hours ahead of Los Angeles.

TEMPERATURE

JAN	FEB	MAR	APR	MAY	JUN	JUL	AUG	SEP	OCT	NOV	DEC
6°C	7°C	12°C	16°C	20°C	23°C	25°C	26°C	21°C	16°C	10°C	7°C
43°F	45°F	54°F	61°F	68°F	73°F	77°F	79°F	70°F	61°F	50°F	45°F

Spring (April, May) takes time to get going. Things don't usually warm up until mid-May.
Summer (June to August) can be glorious. Days are longest in June, with the most sunshine and a pleasant temperature. It is usually hot and sunny in July, and often hot, humid and stormy in August.
Autumn (September to November) has crisp days and usually clear skies.
Winter (December to March) is rarely below freezing but it rains frequently, sometimes with hail, in January and March.

WHAT'S ON

January/February *Chinese New Year:* In Chinatown, 13th *arrondissement.*
April/May *International Paris Fair:* Consumer heaven at Porte de Versailles, foire deparis.fr.
Paris marathon: Starts from the Champs-Élysées, schneiderelectric parismarathon.com.
May *Labour Day* (1 May): Parades and symbolic lily-of-the-valley bouquets.
La Nuit des Musées: On one Saturday evening museums fling their doors open with music, drama and readings.
June *Paris Jazz Festival* (mid-Jun to Jul): Weekends

at Parc Floral de Paris (parisjazzfestival.fr).
Fête de la Musique (21 Jun): Music on the streets.
La Marche des Fiertés LGBT de Paris (Gay Pride) (Sat in late Jun): Popular procession, plus partying in the Marais district.
July *Bastille Day* (14 Jul): The most important French festival celebrates the 1789 storming of the Bastille. Fireworks and street dances on the evening of the 13th and a parade on the 14th on the Champs-Élysées.
July–August *Paris Quartier d'Été:* Outdoor perfor-mances, quartierdete.com.
Paris Plages: Beaches

along the quays of the Seine.
September *Festival d'Automne à Paris* (mid-Sep to Dec): Music, theater and dance all over the city, festival-automne.com.
October *Foire Internationale d'Art Contemporain:* Paris's biggest modern art fair, fiacparis.com.
Nuit Blanche: For one night various cultural venues open all night, free.
November *Beaujolais Nouveau* (third Thu in Nov): Drinking in all the city's bars.
December *Paris International Boat Show* salonnautiqueparis.com.

PARIS ONLINE

visitparisregion.com

The website of the Paris Île de France regional tourist authority has a huge quantity and variety of information on Paris and the surrounding region, including entertainment and events, shopping, sport and leisure, children's Paris, accommodations and public transportation. It now has a new site dedicated to English-language speakers.

parisinfo.com

The Paris Tourist Office online has listings and practical information, sightseeing and links to other useful sites covering every aspect of leisure in the city. It also provides an online hotel booking service.

parisbymouth.com

Information for foodies, or someone looking for the latest hot bistro, rising star chef or up-coming food festivals in the city.

parisvoice.com

Intended for English-speaking Parisians, this site gives an insider's view of the city, with features, events information, restaurant reviews, classified ads, a Q&A column (dealing with some very serious issues) and more.

paris.fr

The official site of Paris's mayor and city council has information on museums, theaters, parks and sport, as well as a virtual tour of the Hôtel de Ville. There is also a wealth of civic news aimed at Paris residents.

france.fr

The official website for the French tourist authority has information for the whole of France, but Paris features heavily. Find the latest exhibition and concert information, plus practical information about your stay in France.

paris-update.com

What's happening, updated weekly: art shows, films, restaurants, concerts.

TRAVEL SITES

parisdigest.com
Independent guide showing you around the city and providing mainstream practical information. A good range of hotel, restaurant and shopping guides.

fodors.com
A complete travel-planning site. You can research prices; book air tickets, cars and rooms; ask questions (and get answers) from fellow travelers; and find links to other sites.

PARIS WIFI

There is free access to WiFi in almost 300 parks, libraries and public buildings in Paris. Hot spots are shown with distinctive oval signs. You'll need to link to PARIS_WI-FI_ page, select your pass, create a password, fill in a form and agree to terms. Each free session lasts up to 2 hours.

Getting There

GETTING YOUR BEARINGS

Think of Paris as a snail, with its shell curling around the 1st *arrondissement* (district) right in the middle. The numbers of the other *arrondissements* follow clockwise, ending with the 20th on the eastern side of the city. *C'est logique, non?*

AIRPORTS

Most international flights arrive at Roissy Charles de Gaulle airport, with some international and French domestic flights arriving at Orly airport. Paris has good rail connections, including the Eurostar train direct from London.

Roissy Charles de Gaulle Airport
Bus 50 mins, €11
Train 35 min, €10

Orly Airport
Bus 30 min, €12.50

60km (40 miles)

FROM ROISSY CHARLES DE GAULLE

Roissy (tel 3950, outside France 331 70 36 39 50, adp.fr) is 23km (14 miles) northeast of central Paris and has three terminals. Air France currently operates out of Terminal 2. There are three ways to get to the city.

By bus: Air France (cars-airfrance.com) operates a bus service (Line 4) between the airport and Montparnasse and Gare de Lyon, every 30 minutes 6am–10pm (€17.50), and to the Arc de Triomphe (Étoile) and Porte Maillot (Line 2) every 20–30 minutes, 5.45am–11pm (€17). You can buy tickets from the driver or at the Air France offices in the terminal. Or take the 50-minute trip on Roissybus that runs every 15 or 20 minutes from Terminals 1, 2 and 3 to Opéra 6am–12.30am (€11).

By train: The RER (Réseau Express Régional) Line B takes around 35 minutes to central Paris (€10). Trains leave every 10–15 minutes.

By taxi: A taxi costs around €50–70 (confirm the price with the driver before setting off) and takes between 30 minutes and 1 hour, depending on traffic. Allow for a 15 percent increase in fares at night, on Sundays and public holidays.

FROM ORLY

Orly (tel 3950, outside France 331 70 36 39 50, adp.fr), the smaller of Paris's two main international airports, is 14km (8.5 miles) from central Paris with no direct train to the city.

By bus: Air France provides shuttle buses to Les Invalides, Etoile and Gare Montparnasse every 20–30 minutes 6am–11.40pm (€12.50). The trip takes about 30 minutes.

By train: The Orlyval train, which operates daily 6am–11pm, will take you to Antony, where you can change for Line B of the RER rail system (€12.05). From here it's around 25 minutes to central Paris.

By taxi: A taxi costs around €45 (make sure you confirm the price before setting off) and takes 15–30 minutes. Allow for a 15 percent increase in fares at night, on Sundays and on public holidays.

EUROSTAR

The Eurostar (tel 01 70 70 60 88 in France, 03432 186 186 in the UK, eurostar.com) takes you from London to the Gare du Nord in the heart of Paris in about 2 hours 15 minutes. From here there are good Métro and RER connections, or you can take a taxi.

THALYS

Thalys (tel 3635, thalys.com) offers daily high-speed train services linking Paris to Brussels, Antwerp, Amsterdam, Cologne and Dortmund.

BUDGET OPTIONS

Within Europe, low-cost airlines such as easyJet (easyjet.com) and Ryanair (ryanair.com) offer some attractive and competitive prices that can sometimes beat the cost of traveling by train. But the tickets are not always bargains; they are priced according to availability and demand. As always, it is usually best to book as far in advance as possible. Keep in mind that Ryanair flies in and out of Beauvais airport, 70km (43 miles) from Paris, so the low cost of a ticket may not be worth the time lost in traveling to and from the airport. EasyJet uses Roissy Charles de Gaulle airport for flights from the UK.

VISAS AND TRAVEL INSURANCE

Visas are not required for EU, US or Canadian nationals, but you will need a valid passport. (Always check the latest requirements before you travel.) EU citizens receive reduced-cost medical treatment with the European Health Insurance Card (EHIC). Full insurance is still strongly advised and is essential for all other travelers.

Getting Around

Paris has a mixed record on access and amenities. On the Métro, only the Meteor line (No. 14) has easy access for people with disabilities. Since 2009, all 63 bus lines in the city are wheelchair accessible and 80 percent of the bus stops have been specially adapted. Infomobi (☎ 09 70 81 83 85, info-mobi.com) is a service with information and news about public transportation for visitors with a disability. RATP's Les Compagnons du Voyage (☎ 01 58 76 08 33, compagnons.com) provides companions for visitors with disabilities (if not in an electric wheelchair), but for a fee. Two taxi companies, G7 (☎ 01 47 39 00 91, taxisg7.com) and Taxis PMR (☎ 06 14 67 75 02, taxipmr.onlc.fr), will take wheelchairs.

The website of the Paris Tourist Office (parisinfo.com) has information for visitors with disabilities, including a list of accessible sights. The downloadable *Accessible Paris* guide has more information about getting around, and can be accessed on the Paris Tourist Office website (parisinfo.com).

MÉTRO

The best way to travel around Paris is by Métro or RER, two separate but linked systems (ratp.fr). The RER is the suburban line, which passes through the heart of the city. The Métro is the underground system, with 14 main lines and 303 stations. Both are inexpensive and efficient, and free maps of all the routes are available at station ticket windows. Any place is within easy walking distance of a Métro or RER station. Both systems function in the same way and the tickets are interchangeable within the city. It is cheaper to buy a *carnet* of 10 tickets than to buy each ticket separately.

● Métro lines are always identified by their destination and a number; connections are shown in *correspondances* panels displayed on the platform.

● The first Métros run at 5.30am, and the last around 1.15am (2.15am Fri and Sat).

● Keep your ticket until you exit—it has to be re-inserted on the RER, and ticket inspectors prowl the Métro.

TICKETS AND PASSES

● Tickets and passes function for Métro, buses, trams and RER.

● One ticket (€1.80) gives access to zones 1 and 2 of the Métro network, the RER within Paris, trams and Parisian and suburban buses. A *carnet* of 10 tickets is €14.10.

● Single tickets (known as Ticket t+) are only valid for a single journey without changing between bus, Métro, tram and RER.

● Prices of passes and suburban RER tickets depend on how many travel zones you intend to pass through.

● Mobilis is a one-day pass, valid on the Métro, buses and RER.

● A Paris Visite card gives unlimited travel for one, two, three or five days plus discounts at certain monuments, but you need to do a lot of traveling to make it pay.

● *Navigo Découverte* travel cards for visitors are obtainable from stations and valid for a week *(Forfait Navigo Semaine)*, starting Monday and ending the following Sunday, or month *(Forfait Navigo Mois)*. Both are valid on routes from the airports to downtown. You'll need a passport photo and the card itself costs €5.

BATOBUS

Traveling by Batobus—a river shuttle boat—is fun (late-Apr to early Sep daily 10–9.30, every 20 minutes; late-Mar to late-Apr and early Sep to early Nov, Mon–Thu 10–7 every 30 minutes, Fri–Sun 10–9.30, every 25 minutes; early-Nov to late-Mar Mon–Thu 10–5, every 45 minutes, Fri–Sun 10–7, every 30 minutes). It stops at the Eiffel Tower, Musée d'Orsay, Saint-Germain-des-Prés, Notre-Dame, Jardin des Plantes, Hôtel de Ville, Louvre, Champs-Élysées and Beaugrenelle. You can join at any point. An all-day ticket costs €16 (tel 0825 01 01 01, batobus.com).

BICYCLES

Bicycles are available at self-service stations across Paris, as part of the Vélib' hire scheme (tel 01 30 79 79 30, velib.paris.fr). One-day (€1.70) or seven-day (€8) tickets are available; major cards are accepted.

TAXIS

Taxis can be hailed in the street if the roof sign is illuminated or can be found at taxi ranks outside most main attractions. There are three tariffs in central Paris: A applies Mon–Sat 10am–5pm; B applies Mon–Sat 5pm–10am, Sun 7am–midnight and 24 hours on public holidays Mon–Sat; C applies Sun midnight–7am. There are extra charges for the fourth and fifth passengers, and for more than one piece of luggage over 5kg (11 lbs). Tip drivers 10 percent.

● The initial fee for hiring a taxi is €3.83 and the minimum fare is €7. Tariff A is €1.06 per km, B €1.29 and C €1.56. If luggage is more than 5kg (11 lbs) there is an excess of €1.

● Taxi ranks that have telephones can be called on 01 45 30 30 30. Select your *arrondissement* with the help of the voice server, who will connect you to the closest rank.

STUDENT VISITORS

● An International Student Identity Card can reduce cinema charges, entrance to museums and air and rail travel.

● MIJE (Maison Internationale de la Jeunesse et des Étudiants)
✉ 6 rue Fourcy, 75004
☎ 01 42 74 23 45, mije.com
🚇 Saint-Paul
🕐 Daily 7am–1am. Three hostels for young people in the heart of Paris.

● CIDJ (Centre d'Information et de Documentation Jeunesse)
✉ 101 quai Branly, 75015
☎ 01 44 49 29 32, cidj.com
🚇 Bir-Hakeim
🕐 Tue–Fri 1–6, Sat 1–5. Youth information office for jobs, courses, sport.

TOURIST OFFICE

● Office du Tourisme de Paris
✉ 25 rue des Pyramides, 75001
☎ parisinfo.com
🕐 Nov–Apr daily 9–7; May–Oct 10–7 (Sun from 11)
🚇 Pyramides
❓ There are English-speaking staff in the office

Essential Facts

MONEY

The euro is the official currency of France. There are bank notes in denominations of 5, 10, 20, 50, 100, 200 and 500 euros and coins in denominations of 1, 2, 5, 10, 20 and 50 cents and 1 and 2 euros.

TIPPING

In every restaurant, by law, a 15 percent service charge and all relevant taxes are already in the prices on the menu. If the service was especially pleasant, or if you feel odd about leaving nothing, then you can leave another couple of euros or 5 percent. In taxis it is customary to give the driver a 10 percent tip, but only if you are happy with the service.

CREDIT CARDS

● Credit cards are widely accepted.
● VISA cards are the most widely accepted and can be used in cash dispensers. Make sure you know your international PIN. MasterCard and Diners Club are also widely accepted.
● American Express is less common, so Amex cardholders needing cash should use Bureau de Change Kanoo. Offices at 11 rue Scribe, 75009, tel 0153 30 99 00; 64 Boulevard Haussmann, 75009, tel 01 42 82 41 08; 24 rue du Sèvres, 75007, tel 01 42 22 52 07.

ETIQUETTE

● Shake hands on introduction and on leaving; once you know people well replace this with a peck on both cheeks.
● Always use *vous* unless the other person breaks into *tu*.
● It is polite to add *Monsieur, Madame* or *Mademoiselle* when addressing strangers.
● Always say *bonjour* and *au revoir* in shops.
● When calling waiters, use *Monsieur* or *Madame* (not *garçon*).
● Dress carefully. More emphasis is put on appearance in France than in other countries and smart casual dress is the norm.

FOREIGN EXCHANGE

● Only banks with Change signs will change foreign currency/traveler's checks; a passport is necessary. Bureaux de change are open longer hours but rates can be poorer. Fees for cashing euro traveler's checks can be high.
● Airport and station exchange desks are open daily 6 or 6.30am to 10 or 10.30pm.

MEDICINES AND MEDICAL TREATMENT

● Minor ailments can often be treated at pharmacies.
● Public hospitals have a 24-hour emergency service *(urgences)* and specialist doctors. Payment is made on the spot, but if you are hospitalized see the *assistante sociale* to arrange payment through your insurance.
● House calls are made by SOS Médecins, tel 36 24 or 01 47 07 77 77, sosmedecins.fr.

- For dental problems contact SOS Dentaire, tel 01 45 26 15 54, urgence-dentaire-paris. com.
- 24-hour pharmacy: Pharmacie Malesherbes, 84 avenue des Champs-Élysées, 75008, tel 01 45 62 02 41.
- Publicis drugstore (133 avenue des Champs-Élysées, tel 01 47 20 39 25) is a pharmacy, café, newsagent and tobacconist, open until 2am. With a night pharmacy open 2am–8am.
- Pharmacies display a green cross outside.

NATIONAL HOLIDAYS

- 1 January, Easter Monday, 1 May, 8 May, Ascension (a Thursday in May), Whit Monday (late May or early June), 14 July, 15 August, 1 November, 11 November, 25 December.
- Sunday services for public transportation operate; many local shops, restaurants and even large stores disregard national holidays.

POST OFFICES

- Stamps can be bought at *tabacs*; post mail in any yellow mailbox.
- All post offices offer express courier post (Chronopost), and photocopy machines.

PUBLIC TOILETS

- Public toilets are free and generally well maintained, although they are not plentiful.
- The Point WCs, on the Champs-Élysées, at the Carrousel du Louvre, Metro Cluny–La Sorbonne, and on boulevard Haussmann are "super loos," for €1.50.
- Malls and department stores have good public facilities and every café has a toilet, but order a drink too.

EMERGENCY NUMBERS

- Crisis-line in English: SOS Help ☎ 01 46 21 46 46 soshelpline.org
- 🕐 3pm–11pm
- Police ☎ 17
- Any emergency ☎ 112
- Ambulance (SAMU) ☎ 15
- Fire (*sapeurs pompiers*) ☎ 18
- Anti-poison ☎ 01 40 05 48 48
- Police lost-property office ✉ 36 rue des Morillons, 75015 ☎ 08 21 00 25 25

ELECTRICITY

- Voltage is 220V; French sockets take plugs with two round pins.

EMBASSIES/CONSULATES

US Embassy	✉ 2 avenue Gabriel, 75008 ☎ 01 43 12 22 22
US Consulate	✉ 4 avenue Gabriel, 75008 ☎ 01 43 12 22 22
Canadian Embassy	✉ 35 avenue Montaigne, 75008 ☎ 01 44 43 29 00
British Embassy	✉ 35 rue du Faubourg Saint-Honoré, 75008 ☎ 01 44 51 31 00
British Consulate	✉ 16 rue d'Anjou, 75008 ☎ 01 44 51 31 00
Australian Embassy	✉ 4 rue Jean-Rey, 75015 ☎ 01 40 59 33 00
New Zealand Embassy	✉ 103 rue de Grenelle, 75007 ☎ 01 45 01 43 43

OPENING HOURS

● Banks: Mon–Fri 9–12.30, 2–5. Closed on public holidays and often the pre-ceding afternoon.
● Post offices: Mon–Fri 8–7, Sat 8–12. The main post office (✉ 52 rue du Louvre, 75001) is closed for renovations until 2018.
● Shops: Mon–Sat 9–7 or 10–8. Some close Mon and an hour at lunch.
● Museums: National museums close on Tue, municipal museums on Mon. Individual opening hours vary.

PRESS

● Main dailies are *Le Monde* (serious, centrist), *Libération* (left-wing) and *Le Figaro* (right-wing).
● For weekly listings of cultural events, buy a copy of *Pariscope* (the most pop-ular listings magazine) or *L'Officiel des Spectacles* (offi.fr).
● Central newspaper kiosks and newsagents stock European dailies (widely available on the day of issue) and *USA Today*.
● Visit trouverlapresse.com to find out exactly where you can buy your favorite publication.

SENSIBLE PRECAUTIONS

● Watch wallets and handbags as pickpockets are active, particularly in busy bars, flea markets, cinemas, the Métro, rail stations and the airport.
● Ticket touts operate at train and Métro stations. Buy from machines or ticket kiosks.
● Keep the numbers of your traveler's-check separate from the checks.
● It is important to make a declaration at a local *commissariat* (police station) to claim losses on your insurance.
● Women are generally safe traveling alone or together, although the same risks apply as in any city in western Europe. Deal with any unwanted attention firmly and politely. Avoid the Métro late at night.

TELEPHONES

● Most phone booths use Orange cards (*télécarte* for 50 or 120 units), sold at post offices, *tabacs* or main Métro stations.
● To call France from the US, dial 011 33, then leave out the first zero. To call the US from France dial 00 1 followed by the number.
● To call France from the UK, dial 00 33—omit the first zero from the number. To call the UK from France, dial 00 44—omit the first zero.
● All numbers in the Île-de-France, including Paris, start with 01 unless they are premium rate, when they start with 08; some are toll-free.
● Numbers in the French provinces begin with: 02 Northwest, 03 Northeast, 04 Southeast, 05 Southwest.

TICKETS

● The Paris Museum Pass (parismuseum pass.fr) gives access to 54 museums. It is valid for two, four or six consecutive days. You can buy it online or at tourist offices, museums and Fnac stores.
● Paris Passlib' is available from tourist offices across Paris. It offers entry to over 50 museums and monuments plus reductions at other attrac-tions, a river cruise, Big Bus tour and all public transportation costs for a period of two, three, or five consecutive days.

Words and Phrases

BASIC VOCABULARY

oui/non	yes/no
s'il vous plaît	please
merci	thank you
excusez-moi	excuse me
pardon	I'm sorry
bonjour	hello, good morning
bonsoir	good evening
au revoir	good-bye
de rien/avec plaisir	you're welcome
parlez-vous anglais?	do you speak English?
je ne comprends pas	I don't understand
combien?	how much?
trop cher	too expensive
je voudrais…	I'd like…
où est/sont…?	where is/are…?
ici/là	here/there
tournez à gauche/droite	turn left/right
tout droit	straight on
quand?	when?
aujourd'hui	today
hier	yesterday
demain	tomorrow
combien de temps?	how long?
à quelle heure?	at what time?
à quelle heure ouvrez/fermez-vous?	what time do you open/close?
avez-vous…?	do you have…?
une chambre simple	a single room
une chambre double	a double room
avec/sans salle de bains	with/without bathroom
le petit déjeuner	breakfast
le déjeuner	lunch
le dîner	dinner
c'est combien?	how much is this?
puis-je réserver une table	I'd like to book a table
une bouteille/un verre de…	a bottle/glass of…
acceptez-vous des cartes de crédit?	do you take credit cards?
j'ai besoin d'un médecin/dentiste	I need a doctor/dentist
pouvez-vous m'aider?	can you help me?
où est l'hôpital?	where is the hospital?
où est le commissariat?	where is the police station?

NUMBERS

un	1
deux	2
trois	3
quatre	4
cinq	5
six	6
sept	7
huit	8
neuf	9
dix	10
onze	11
douze	12
treize	13
quatorze	14
quinze	15
seize	16
dix-sept	17
dix-huit	18
dix-neuf	19
vingt	20
vingt-et-un	21
trente	30
quarante	40
cinquante	50
soixante	60
soixante-dix	70
quatre-vingts	80
quatre-vingt-dix	90
cent	100
mille	1,000

MONTHS

janvier	January
février	February
mars	March
avril	April
mai	May
juin	June
juillet	July
août	August
septembre	September
octobre	October
novembre	November
décembre	December

Index

The Automobile Association would like to thank the following photographers, companies and picture libraries for their assistance in the preparation of this book.

2i Paris Tourist Office/Marc Bertrand; 2ii AA/K Blackwell; 2iii AA/K Blackwell; 2iv Hemis/Alamy; 2v AA/ M Jourdan; 3i AA/K Blackwell; 3ii AA/K Blackwell; 3iii AA/K Blackwell; 3iv AA/K Blackwell; 4 AA/K Blackwell; 5 Paris Tourist Office/Marc Bertrand; 6/7t AA/K Blackwell; 6/7ct PARAMOUNT/ THE KOBAL COLLECTION; 6/7cb THE KOBAL COLLECTION; 6/7b Kristjan Porm/Alamy; 7ct AA/K Blackwell; 7cb MGM/THE KOBAL COLLECTION; 8/9t AA/K Blackwell; 8c AA/K Blackwell; 8/9b AA/K Paterson; 9ct AA/K Blackwell; 9cb AA/M Jourdan; 10l AA/K Blackwell; 10r The Bridgeman Art Library; 11 Keystone/Getty Images; 12 AA/K Blackwell; 14 AA/K Blackwell; 15tl AA/K Blackwell; 15cl AA/K Blackwell; 15tr AA/K Blackwell; 15cr AA/K Blackwell; 16l Centre Pompidou; 16t AA/T Souter; 16/17 Susana Vázquez; 17l AA/C Sawyer; 17tr Susana Vázquez; 17cr Centre Pompidou; 18t AA/K Blackwell; 18b AA/K Blackwell; 19tl AA/K Blackwell; 19cl AA/K Blackwell; 19r AA/K Blackwell; 20l AA/K Blackwell; 20/21t AA/K Blackwell; 20c AA/K Blackwell; 21c AA/K Blackwell; 21r AA/M Jourdan; 22l AA/M Jourdan; 22tr AA 22cr AA/K Blackwell; 23tl AA/K Blackwell; 23cl AA/K Blackwell; 23r AA/K Blackwell; 24/25 age fotostock/Alamy; 25tr AA/C Sawyer; 25cr AA/K Blackwell; 26l AA/K Blackwell; 26/27t AA/K Blackwell; 26/27c AA/K Blackwell; 27t AA/K Blackwell; 27c AA/K Blackwell; 28 AA/K Blackwell; 29t AA/M Jourdan; 29c AA/K Blackwell; 29r AA/J Tims; 30l AA/M Jourdan; 30/31t AA/M Jourdan; 30/31c AA/J Tims; 31t The Bridgeman Art Library; 31c Susana Vázquez; 32 AA/J Tims; 33tl AA/K Blackwell; 33t AA/K Blackwell; 33c AA/K Blackwell; 34 AA/C Sawyer; 34/35t AA/K Paterson; 34/35c AA/M Jourdan; 35t AA/M Jourdan; 35c AA/K Paterson; 36 AA/K Blackwell; 36/37 AA/K Blackwell; 37t imageBROKER/Alamy; 37cr AA/K Blackwell; 38l AA/M Jourdan; 38/9t Danita Delimont/Alamy; 38/9b Paris Le Marais/Alamy; 39r AA/P Kenward; 40 AA/K Blackwell; 41tl Giraudon/The Bridgeman Art Library; 41cl The Art Archive/ Alamy; 41r Hemis/Alamy; 42 AA/K Blackwell; 42/43t AA/M Jourdan; 42/43c AA/K Blackwell; 43t AA/B Rieger; 43cl AA/K Blackwell; 43cr AA/K Blackwell; 44 AA/K Blackwell; 45tl AA/K Blackwell; 45cl AA/K Blackwell; 45c Dorothy Alexander/Alamy; 45r AA/K Blackwell; 46/47 AA/K Blackwell; 47l AA/K Blackwell; 47r AA/M Jourdan; 48 AA/T Souter 48/49t AA/K Blackwell; 48/49c AA/M Jourdan; 49 AA/K Blackwell; 50l AA/K Blackwell; 50r AA/K Blackwell; 50/51 AA/K Blackwell; 51l AA/K Blackwell; 51t AA/M Jourdan; 51c AA/K Blackwell; 52 AA/C Sawyer; 53l AA/P Kenward; 53t Paris Tourist Office/Marc Bertrand; 53c Andrew Duke/Alamy; 54l AA/K Blackwell; 54r Glenn Harper/Alamy; 54/55 Jon Arnold Images Ltd/Alamy; 55 JOHN KELLERMAN/Alamy; 56 AA/K Blackwell; 56/57t AA/K Blackwell; 56c AA/K Blackwell; 57l AA/K Blackwell; 57tr AA/J Tims; 57cr AA/J Tims; 58 AA/T Souter; 58/59 AA/K Blackwell; 59tl AA/K Blackwell; 59tr AA/K Blackwell; 59cr AA/K Blackwell; 60 AA/K Blackwell; 60/61t AA/K Blackwell; 60/61c AA/K Blackwell; 61t AA/K Blackwell; 61c AA/K Blackwell; 62 AA/K Blackwell; 63tl AA/K Blackwell; 63c AA/M Jourdan; 63tc AA/K Blackwell; 63tr Hemis/Alamy; 64 AA/K Blackwell; 66l AA/K Blackwell; 66r AA/K Blackwell; 67l AA/K Blackwell; 67r AA/K Blackwell; 68 AA/K Blackwell; 69l AA/C Sawyer; 69r AA/K Blackwell; 70l AA/K Blackwell; 70r AA/K Blackwell; 71l JOHN KELLERMAN/Alamy; 71r AA/K Blackwell; 72 AA/K Blackwell; 73l AA/C Sawyer; 73r AA/M Jourdan; 74l AA/M Jourdan; 74r AA/T Souter; 75l AA/C Sawyer; 75r AA/K Blackwell; 76 AA/K Blackwell; 77l AA/D Noble; 77r AA/D Noble; 78l Disney Enterprises, Inc; 78r Disney Enterprises, Inc; 79 AA/D Noble; 80 Hemis/Alamy; 82t AA/K Blackwell; 82b AA/J Tims; 83t AA/K Blackwell; 83b AA/K Blackwell; 86i imageBROKER/Alamy; 86ii AA/K Blackwell; 86iii AA/M Jourdan; 86iv AA/K Blackwell; 87 AA/K Blackwell; 88t Christophe Testi/Alamy; 88b AA/K Blackwell; 89t AA/K Blackwell; 89b AA/C Sawyer; 92i AA/K Blackwell; 92ii AA/K Blackwell; 92iii AA/K Paterson; 92iv AA/K Blackwell; 92v AA/K Blackwell; 92vi AA/K Blackwell; 94t AA/M Jourdan 94b AA/M Jourdan; 95 AA/K Blackwell; 98i Centre Pompidou; 98ii AA/M Jourdan; 98iii AA/K Blackwell; 98iv Paris Tourist Office/Amélie Dupont; 100 AA/K Blackwell; 101t AA/K Blackwell; 101b AA/K Blackwell; 104i AA/K Blackwell; 104ii AA/K Blackwell; 104iii AA/K Blackwell; 104iv AA/J Tims; 104v AA/K Blackwell; 104vi AA/M Jourdan 106t AA/P Enticknap; 106b AA/M Jourdan; 107t AA/J Tims; 107b AA/P Enticknap; 110t AA/T Souter; 110b AA/J Tims; 111l AA/K Blackwell; 111r AA/M Jourdan; 112t AA/M Jourdan; 112c AA/K Blackwell; 112b AA/M Jourdan; 113t AA/K Blackwell; 113c AA/M Jourdan; 116i AA/K Blackwell; 116ii AA/K Blackwell; 116iii AA/K Blackwell; 116iv AA/K Blackwell; 117 AA/K Blackwell; 118 AA/M Jourdan; 120/121t Paris Tourist Office/Marc Bertrand; 120/121ct Paris Tourist Office/David Lefranc; 121ct AA/C Sawyer; 120cb AA/C Sawyer; 120/121cb AA/C Sawyer; 120/121b AA/C Sawyer; 125 AA/C Sawyer; 127 AA/K Blackwell; 128 AA/K Blackwell; 130 AA/K Blackwell; 132/133t Paris Tourist Office/David Lefranc; 132ct Paris Tourist Office/David Lefranc; 132/133ct AA/K Blackwell; 132/133cb Paris Tourist Office/Amélie Dupont; 133cb AA/P Enticknap; 132b AA/K Paterson; 133b AA/K Blackwell; 140 AA/K Blackwell; 142i AA/C Sawyer; 142ii AA/K Blackwell; 142iii AA/K Blackwell; 142iv AA/K Blackwell; 144 AA/K Blackwell; 147 AA/K Blackwell; 148 AA/K Blackwell; 150 AA/C Sawyer; 152 AA/K Blackwell; 154i AA/K Blackwell; 154ii Courtesy of Dorchester Collection; 154iii AA/C Sawyer; 154iv Courtesy of Dorchester Collection; 160 AA/K Blackwell.

Every effort has been made to trace the copyright holders, and we apologize in advance for any unintentional omissions or errors. We would be pleased to apply any corrections in a following edition of this publication.